geography 3–11

Also available

Science 5–11: A Guide for Teachers
Alan Howe, Dan Davies, Kendra McMahon, Lee Towler and Tonie Scott
1-84312-319-3

MFL 5–11: Issues for Teachers
Jane Jones and Simon Coffey
1-84312-390-8

geography 3–11

a guide for teachers

Edited by Hilary Cooper, Chris Rowley
and Simon Asquith

David Fulton Publishers

David Fulton Publishers Ltd
The Chiswick Centre, 414 Chiswick High Road, London W4 5TF

www.fultonpublishers.co.uk

First published in Great Britain in 2006 by David Fulton Publishers

10 9 8 7 6 5 4 3 2 1

David Fulton Publishers is a division of Granada Learning Limited.

British Library Cataloguing in Publication Data
A catalogue record for this book is available from the British Library.

ISBN: 1 84312 421 1   (EAN: 978 1843124214)

Typeset by RefineCatch Ltd, Bungay, Suffolk
Printed and bound in Great Britain

Contents

Preface

Why did we write this book?

A shared philosophy

Essentially all the contributors to this book believe in an holistic approach to child development, valuing the social and emotional as well as cognitive dimensions. We also respect the importance of teachers understanding the key concepts and skills of each subject and being articulate about its distinctive importance. We recognise the considerable skills of teachers in being able to translate this understanding into activities which will promote the all-round development of children of different ages and abilities. Professional expertise involves the ability to create an ethos in which children feel able, and indeed motivated, to ask questions, which are real and meaningful to them, and to be supported in finding out how to answer them. We believe that education takes place when teachers and pupils are engaged in mutually stimulating, shared enquiries and discussions.

By now you may be saying that you remember the days when most teachers shared this philosophy – or maybe you are not, if you have only experienced grappling with the constant government initiatives of recent years. In either case, read on!

A challenge

We felt empowered to write this book, inspired by the QCA Futures: Meeting the Challenge programme. I was invited to attend a 'Summit' – no less – held to launch the programme at the Cumberland Hotel in London on 13 January 2005. We had been sent in advance a collection of papers by leading educationists on liberating approaches to 'the forces of change'. Tim Brighouse, Chief Adviser for London schools, emphasised the importance of 'experience'. He criticised the 'monotonous, metronomic nature of a timetabled curriculum' and said schools should have planned series of days or weeks which heighten readiness to learn. John White, Emeritus

Professor of Philosophy at London University Institute of Education said that education is about the sort of person education is meant to foster – 'someone who values personal relationships, is a responsible and caring citizen, able to manage risk and committed to sustainable development'. He recognised that understanding history, geography and science is an essential part of understanding the world around you, but said that the starting point should be whole-person aims. 'The next step,' he said, 'is to work out how one learns wholeheartedness, co-operating in a team, sensitivity to issues of global citizenship'. Sara Parkin, programme director of Forum for the Future, focused on sustainable literacy. Professor Jean Ruddock's paper, 'Pupil voices here to stay', stressed the importance of teachers talking with pupils about things that matter. Lesley Longstone, Director of the DfES International Strategy, dealt with the global dimension and its importance for subjects. These papers can be found on the QCA website (www.qca.org.uk/futures/).

All of this provided a backdrop for discussing what forces for change should influence dynamic curriculum development to meet the needs of our time and how to allow scope for innovation and personalisation in learning. Then we moved into groups to discuss the implications for each subject.

The geography group saw its response to 'the forces of change' as identifying its distinctive contribution of 'big ideas', within broad, overarching aims of the whole curriculum, and with controlled and constructive cross-disciplinary contributions. The 'big ideas' were defined as geographical imagination, spatial awareness, interdependence, links between the personal and global, and environmental interaction. Key distinctive experiences included valuing and building on pupils' own experiences, promoting an active and critical approach to enquiry, contributing to political literacy by exploring the values dimension of issues, promoting social awareness and social and emotional development through fieldwork and address-ing real questions and issues. The group recommended examples showing how this can be put into practice. Some challenge!

Diverse experience

We felt that our shared philosophy of education and the special approaches to the teaching and learning of geography developed, in particular by Chris Rowley and Chris Buxton, were very much in tune with these recommendations. They are both passionate about their subject. They have been downhearted by its marginalisation as the emphasis on literacy and numeracy has devalued it, almost to the point of extinction in some schools. Teachers are expected to teach it in school but there has been no requirement to include geography in their training courses and virtually no in-service training. Hardly surprising then that recent inspection reports have found it to be the worst taught subject in the curriculum. Chris (with the beard) Rowley and Chris (without the beard) Buxton were at first sceptical, but became keen to lead the team in responding to the challenge which the Futures Programme offered.

How we wrote the book

Colleagues in the Faculty of Education at St Martin's have written a number of collaborative books on current issues and concerns. We are all busy people but find that writing a chapter in a book with a common theme is manageable, encourages us to reflect upon our own practice and to work with children and teachers in schools.

September 2004

We discussed the possibility of a book with Tracey Alcock, publisher for initial teacher training textbooks at David Fulton. 'You need to wait until the Geographical Association has published its new Handbook,' she said, 'so that you can make links with it where appropriate. You also need chapters on key aspects such as planning, place, inclusion, the global dimension, but within that structure, be creative!'

October–December 2004

We wrote chapter titles and invited colleagues with specialist expertise in each area to contribute a chapter. The team met to agree key ideas which would run through and characterise the book: enquiry, values, issues, cross-curricular dimensions. This was a really enjoyable meeting of colleagues who do not usually work closely together, thrashing out some mutually interesting problems from different perspectives; for example, How do you get children to ask questions? Does it matter if they come up with 'wrong' ideas? How do you handle this? At the end of December we sent off the proposal.

February 2005

Chris Rowley and Simon Asquith presented a paper on our proposed book at the Charney Manor Primary Conference, asking for comments and suggestions. The proposal was reviewed for David Fulton by members of the geographical community. We built all their suggestions into a revised proposal, which was accepted. Hurray!

February 2005–March 2006

Chapters were drafted, discussed with editors, revised, etc. I kept an eye on the overall shape of the book and its required format. Chris Rowley did a sterling job as geography consultant to colleagues. Manuscript to publisher. Copy-editing, typesetting, Index. So you see, it has been a long time in coming!

Over to you

We hope that this book encourages you to take a fresh look at geography and in some ways see it in a new light. We have organised the chapters around key questions resulting from team discussions, partly because we were interested in reflecting on these ourselves and also so that you, the reader, can reflect on, and we hope build on them, in the light of your own experiences. We hope that you enjoy our book and that you and your children have fun. Education is for Enjoyment – that's official!

Hilary Cooper
April 2006

Acknowledgements

The editors are grateful to the many schools and the other organisations involved in working with the chapter authors. Our aim has been that the book should be rooted in experience, that we should reflect together on that experience and consider how it could be developed to reflect current concerns, regarding which we identified the following:

- taking the needs and interests of the child as a starting point;
- making links between geography and other areas of learning and experience, including the spiritual and aesthetic;
- making personal links with children in other places;
- challenging children's thinking through considering value-laden issues; and
- new kinds of geographical enquiry.

The various schools and organisations have helped us, in many different ways, to explore these questions. All the children's names have been changed in the text.

The innovative approaches to enquiry in Chapter 2 are developed from Chris Rowley's work with schools in the Morecambe Bay partnership and with Lisa Strange and the children of Staveley Church of England School, Cumbria. Planning issues in Chapter 3 draw on work on geographical enquiry with the Morcambe Bay partnership schools.

Chris Buxton's Chapter 4, focusing on fieldwork, draws on his work with a number of organisations: with Michelle Donoghue and Jonathan Walkingshaw on the Cumbrian John Muir Award Scheme, with Catherine Mole and the Forest Schools, with Ruth Suddaby and Jayne Buchanen at United Utilities, with Gina Mullarkey at the Cumbrian Development Education Centre, with Kate Jordan and Adrian Letts on the Going Global at Grizedale Project and with Tania Crocket at the Grizedale Education Service. This work also involved many teachers and children: Norma Bagot and Clare Reagan at Fell View Primary, John Nixon and Alison Boyd at Moor Row Primary, Tim Coleman and Alison Wild at Tebay Community School, Laura

Watson at Lowther Endowed School, Ruth Suddaby at Greystoke Primary School, Danielle Metcalfe and Heather Troughton, primary geography specialist students at St Martin's College.

In writing Chapter 5, Nigel Toye worked with the class teacher, Sue Toye, and the head teacher, Nadine Scot, at Hornby Primary School in Cumbria. Denise Evans is grateful to Sheila Marchant, the head teacher at Broad Oak Primary School in Manchester, to Balqis Jamil, the teacher with whom she worked, and to her teaching assistant Paula Davenport, who gave valuable input into the drama sessions.

Acknowledgements and thanks for their contribution to Chapter 6 go to Nicole Gurvedi, the Year 2 class teacher at Marion Richardson School, Stepney, and to Sally Newton, the school's Special Educational Needs Co-ordinator.

Chapter 7 draws on Sophie Mackay's work with postgraduate student teachers Angela Mui, Laura Murphy, Ciara Gosgrave and Ruth Wheeler, working in Harbinger Primary School and Seven Mills Primary School, both on the Isle of Dogs in London. They were working on the Local Action, Global Impact Project. Gina Mullarkey and Vimala John worked with pupils in the Barrow and the Preston Pupil Referral Units. Jan Ashbridge thanks the Reception children in her class during 2004/5 at St Mary's CE Primary School in Kirby Lonsdale, Cumbria, for helping her with Chapter 8.

Kevin Hamel and Kath Langley-Hamel worked on story, music, drama and ICT for Chapter 9 with Denise Gallagher, head teacher, and Kirstie Allerton, class teacher, at Grayrigg School in Cumbria and with Pauline Coates, head teacher, and Matthew Langley, class teacher, at Plymouth Grove Primary School in Manchester. Kath and Kevin are also grateful to John Taylor and to Sam Maitland, the musician, and to Zozo Shuaibu, musician and storyteller, who worked with them on storytelling, geography and music. They also thank Cumbria Learning Support Music (www.tuned-in.org). Mark Squires, head teacher, and the pupils and teachers at Langdale School, and Cath Lawler and Class 4 at Eaglesfield Paddle School in Cumbria made contributions to Chapter 10.

Thanks are also due to many colleagues in the geography community who read draft sections of the book and offered their very helpful comments to the authors. We are grateful to all of them.

The poem in Chapter 10, page 153, is reproduced with the permission of Martin Robertson from the volume *A Hot Bath at Bedtime*, now out of print; website reference http://rtnl.org.uk/now_and_then/.

About the contributors

Jan Ashbridge is currently Senior Lecturer in Early Childhood Education at St Martin's College. Previously she was a class teacher and an advisory teacher for Cumbria Local Education Authority. She wrote the chapter 'Weather girls and boys', which can be found in *Exploring Time and Place Through Play* (David Fulton Publishers, 2004: 142–56).

Simon Asquith is a lecturer in geography and environmental education at St Martin's College and is also the College Partnership Manager for Initial Teacher Education. Prior to this he co-ordinated Primary Geographical and Environmental Education at Liverpool Hope University where he taught on undergraduate and postgraduate geography programmes. He was geography co-ordinator in a number of primary schools. Simon has written regularly for *Primary Geographer* magazine and has written or contributed to a number of books relating to primary geography, including the Curriculum Bank series (Scholastic) and *Oxford Primary Geography* (Oxford University Press).

Chris Buxton is a geography graduate with postgraduate qualifications in geography and outdoor education and in human ecology. He has had extensive experience of working with primary and secondary pupils through Outward Bound, the Youth Hostels Association and Adventure Experience and the Lake District National Park Service. He is currently Senior Lecturer in geography education at St Martin's College.

Hilary Cooper is Professor of History and Pedagogy at St Martin's College. Previously she lectured at Goldsmith's College, University of London. She taught for many years across the 3–11 age range in a variety of London schools and has published widely.

Denise Evans is Senior Lecturer in Drama in Education at St Martin's College. Along with colleagues Nigel Toye and Francis Prendiville, she teaches both students and experienced teachers. Her teaching career has involved working in both primary and secondary schools in Manchester. Prior to taking up her post at St Martin's she was Senior Lecturer at Manchester Metropolitan University.

John Goodwin trained as a teacher specialising in geography. After teaching in a number of schools he is now Senior Lecturer in mathematics education but maintains his interest in the teaching and learning of geography.

Kevin Hamel is currently adviser in music education for Cumbria Local Education Authority after teaching in primary schools and in higher education. He has recently been instrumental in developing the 'tuned-in.org' website to support non-specialist music teachers in primary schools. He has a particular interest in developing children's knowledge and understanding in the foundation subjects through story and music.

Vimala John was born and brought up in West Malaysia and came to Britain in the early 1980s to work in the health sector. Vimala's particular interests are diversity and anti-racist education which are the key themes of 'Keeping Diversity on Track', a project she is currently working on. She has also been a key team member in the Oxfam-funded Philosophy for Global Citizenship project and co-leads SAPERE (Society to Advance Philosophical Enquiry and Reflection in Education) Accredited Level 1 Philosophy for Children courses. Vimala has actively supported teachers across the county of Cumbria in the delivery of the Global Dimension within the curriculum.

Katherine Langley-Hamel currently lectures in English education but has extensive experience in primary schools where her commitment to cross-curricular approaches reflected a desire to make all subjects accessible to all.

Sophie Mackay is a qualified teacher who works at the Humanities Education Centre in Tower Hamlets. She supports primary schools in including the global dimension in the curriculum. She has previously worked as a researcher and visiting lecturer in children's literature at Roehampton University. She co-authored, with Cynthia Ashcroft, 'Story tents: an oracy and global learning project', in *Exploring Time and Place Through Play* (David Fulton, 2004: 109–16).

Gina Mullarkey worked as a primary teacher and outdoor education tutor before joining Cumbria Development Education Centre (CDEC) as a Project Worker in the Barrow area of Cumbria. Gina launched the CDEC local base in 2001 to promote development education and global awareness in schools. Recent work has explored the use of Philosophy for Children to deliver the Global Citizenship Curriculum with students at a local Pupil Referral Unit.

Chris Rowley is Senior Lecturer in environmental and geographical education at St Martin's College. This follows 13 years teaching in Yorkshire, Northumberland and Lincolnshire. He was a member of the committee of SAPERE from 1997 to 2003. An interest in children's understanding of the environment led him to work with teachers around Morecambe Bay between 2003 and 2004 to co-produce the book *Thinking on the Edge* (Lewis and Rowley, Living Earth, 2003).

Neil Simco originally specialised in primary geography education and worked in primary schools. He is currently Dean of the Faculty of Education at St Martin's College.

Justine Slaymaker was a class teacher in Tower Hamlets primary schools for eight years. In her last school she worked closely with the school Special Educational Needs Co-ordinator to establish an on-site resource centre to support children with learning difficulties in developing early literacy, mathematics, play and social skills. Since September 2002 she has lectured on inclusion at St Martin's College London Campus.

Nigel Toye is Senior Lecturer in drama at St Martin's College, Lancaster, responsible for the drama courses on all campuses. He teaches undergraduates, postgraduates and experienced teachers. This follows 16 years teaching in Hertfordshire, including advisory work. Publications include *Drama and Traditional Story for the Early Years* (RoutledgeFalmer, 2000) written in collaboration with Francis Prendiville.

The Hunting of the Snark: An Agony in Eight Fits

By Lewis Carroll

The Bellman's Speech

He had brought a large map representing the sea,

Without the least vestige of land

And the crew were much pleased when they found it to be

A map they could all understand.

'What's the good of Mercator's North Poles and Equators,

Tropics, Zones and Meridian lines?'

So the Bellman would cry and the crew would reply

'They are merely conventional signs!'

Of course we do not deny the importance of maps, but we also feel that the Bellman's words capture the spirit of children's geography – including the fun!

Theory, practice and research: a rationale for primary geography and overview of recent developments

Simon Asquith

THIS BOOK, *GEOGRAPHY 3–11*, reflects and projects a passion for a strong geographical and environmental education for all children in primary and the early years.

The book's authoring team share a belief that an understanding of relationships between each one of us and the places with which we interact are key to being a successful human being in a sustainable world. The authors share a view that children must want to enquire into their world and that they must challenge themselves and the values that they and others hold that impact on people and places. The better children know their world, the better the child will be and the better the world for it. We therefore need teachers to want to teach geography.

In putting such a book together, the authors have recognised the great challenge facing geography as a subject when contextualised in formal curricula as evident in schools. It is a fundamental tenet of this book that the Primary National Strategy and associated national refocusing on the breadth of the curriculum are providing the context for an exploration of creative, value-based, enquiry-focused and challenging geography for children from the Foundation Stage to the end of Key Stage 2. The book recognises what we know of the ways that children learn and it seats geographical and environmental education within wider, holistic approaches to child development and within notions of an integrated approach to the curriculum. There is a critical recognition that geography comes alive when the learner has ownership of their learning and when the enquiry is powered forward by the learner's own needs and desires to make sense of *their* world.

Primary geography – a time of opportunity

Some exciting reawakenings can be observed among those who teach and commentate on geographical education in England and the wider UK. Recent developments in joining up thinkers, researchers, educational leaders and those who provide curriculum support and teacher development have been increasingly generating a new dawn placing the child back at the centre of geographical learning. Ongoing discussion about the future of geography and other subjects is providing a new focus at the national level.

This book comes at a time of great opportunity for early years and primary geography. Discussion about subject boundaries, and therefore of the 'worth' or relative importance of sometimes competing subject areas, is enjoying a revival and curriculum and learning and teaching debate is increasingly flourishing from the individual school or setting level to the national. Geography stands surer than ever of its vital place in the curriculum and is learning hard lessons that have helped it recognise more of how a truly effective geographical and environmental education is actually gained. The following chapters aim to illustrate a range of approaches that will contribute to such an education.

A context for this book

The book is informed by and founded on the Geographical Association's *Primary Geography Handbook*, published in 2004 and edited by Stephen Scoffham (Scoffham 2004). This highly valuable 'manual' follows and builds upon an earlier, equally important volume edited by Roger Carter (Carter 1998). Both of these handbooks were written by a team of volunteer experts from the world of primary geography.

It is hoped that the chapters that follow complement and extend the various sections of the most recent *Handbook* and that they link where possible with practical examples drawn from active classroom and field practitioners.

Chris Rowley, in Chapter 2, focuses on children and geographical enquiry, linking us to *Handbook* chapters on 'Geographies and Learning' and more specifically to the *Handbook* chapter 'Geographical Enquiry and Investigations' (Dinkele 2004). John Goodwin considers, in Chapter 3, how effective planning is seated in progression in geographical learning, making clear links with the *Handbook*'s chapter 'Planning the Geography Curriculum' (Richardson 2004a).

Fieldwork is celebrated as a vital learning and teaching approach in Chapter 4 when Chris Buxton demonstrates links between fieldwork and geographical education for a sustainable world. Themes from a number of *Handbook* chapters are reflected here with the most obvious link being to the dedicated chapter on fieldwork in the 'Geographical Skills' section (Richardson 2004b). Drama is presented as a creative approach in Chapter 5, with reference into the need for children to learn in an active way and one that delivers real engagement. Here, Nigel Toye and Denise Evans extend lines of argument put forward in a number of chapters, including, very notably, that on 'Geography and the Emotions' (Tanner 2004).

Justine Slaymaker explores the inclusion of all children in a geographical education in Chapter 6, with clear links to the *Handbook*'s chapter 'Geography, Inclusion and Special Needs' (Blow 2004) and the global dimension, introduced in Chapter 7 by Sophie Mackay, Gina Mullarkey and Vimala John perfectly complements Mary Young's *Handbook* chapter, 'Geography and the Global Dimension' (Young 2004).

Three authors explore geography's place within an integrated curriculum in Chapters 8 and 9 which focus on the Foundation Stage and Key Stage 1, followed by an overview of KS2 from Hilary Cooper (Chapter 10). Jan Ashbridge considers Foundation Stage geography in Chapter 8, with obvious links into to the *Handbook* chapter 'Young Children Making Sense of their Place in the World' (Martin and Owens 2004) and this examination continues into and through Key Stage 1 as covered by Kevin and Kath Langley-Hamel in Chapter 9.

Neil Simco concludes the book (Chapter 11) with a reflective chapter built on discussions with the book's authoring team and on the journey that they have taken in preparing the work. This helps him return to the theme of the teacher in the primary school and the early years and the wider contexts of enabling meaningful pupil enquiry-based learning, of realising an integrated curriculum that recognises holistic approaches to children's learning, of value-laden approaches and of the importance of learning in each child's 'real world'.

Chapters identify key questions arising out of the curriculum as framed by the National Curriculum for Geography (DfEE/QCA 1999), the Curriculum Guidance for the Foundation Stage (DfEE/QCA 2000) or the Primary National Strategy (DfES 2003) and link these key questions to the *Handbook*. Where possible, authors illustrate with real examples from the classroom or field, aiming to share approaches that demonstrate good contemporary and often innovative practice.

This book takes for granted that the Geographical Association's *Handbook* is an essential reference for any teacher leading geography as a subject in the primary school or the 'Knowledge and Understanding of the World' area of learning in the Foundation Stage.

A primary geography curriculum

Geography has a long-established 'place' in the curriculum. Subject proponents point to its specific areas on offer with reference to life skills, world knowledge and people and places. Geography offers description and interpretation of our surroundings, whether local to us or more distant (Scoffham 2004) and is a pivotal subject with respect children's learning about environmental sustainability, global citizenship and diversity.

In 1993 Patrick Wiegand told us that 'Geography is good for you. It has a potentially significant role in creating a better world' (Wiegand 1993: 1). Simon Catling closes his chapter in the Geographical Association's *Primary Geography Handbook* by suggesting that

> The vital role of geography in the early years and primary curriculum is to support and enable the development of informed, concerned and responsible members of the local and global community, whose sense of wonder, interest in and fascination with the world about them leads to active engagement in sustaining and improving people's lives in their own places, other environments and across the wider world.
>
> (Catling 2004a: 91)

Geography's greatest claim to a 'place' in the curriculum of young learners is therefore, that as they learn about people in places, children are also learning to *be* people in places (Blyth and Krause 1995) and that as they are doing this values such as international understanding, environmental concern and awareness of the interdependent nature of the world (Martin 1995) can develop seated in a growing self-knowledge and awareness. Authors of chapters in this book advocate a curriculum whereby children engage in affective learning through geographical enquiry, a notion highlighted by subject experts drawn together by the Qualifications and Curriculum Authority (QCA) as a part of their 'Futures' thinking. Increasingly the agenda is returning to learning through children's own experiences, their active and critical involvement in environmental issues and their political and emotional literacy in issues-based enquiry (QCA 2005a).

As with any subject, it is interesting to plot changing emphasis according to *zeitgeist*. In 1992 one list cited geographical education, world studies, the European dimension in education, development education, multicultural education, environment education, human rights education, peace education and citizenship as key initiatives within place study, each in turn spawning individual networks (Wiegand 1992). Since then there has been an inevitable waxing and waning of some of these and an amalgamation of others. Citizenship has become a non-statutory National Curriculum subject at primary. Education for Sustainable Development has attracted recognition as an 'approach' by the QCA and is mapped within and across the National Curriculum, including the Geography orders (DfEE/QCA 1999).

Earlier 'traditions' within geography, for example the 'human-environment', 'regional', 'earth-science' and 'spatial' identified in the mid-1960s (Pattison 1964) still have partial echoes today and one of the risks of having a statutory subject with a declining number of capable subject leaders in primary is that certain less helpful elements of this 'old' geography can re-emerge. By the 1980s the focus was on the three geographical approaches of concern with 'place', the tradition of the 'spatial' and the notion of 'graphicacy' (Bale 1987). It is worth noting that in these years, immediately before the National Curriculum for Geography, Bale was advocating 'that it is from the worlds inside children's heads that school geography should build' (Bale 1987: 30). An avalanche of fascinating research into children's mental maps (Gould and White 1974), their spatial behaviour (Hart 1979) and their representations of place (Blaut and Stea 1974; Blades and Spencer 1986; Wiegand 1992) has informed our understanding of children's geographies and it may now be that the time is ripe for renewing such a focus.

Recent lessons learned

Some teachers have never strayed from the focus on the child and the child's learning, but limits to curriculum space, issues over teacher confidence in the subject, lack of teacher in-service support and shortage of appropriate geographical resources have exerted a heavy price on the quality of geographical learning in primary schools (Catling 2003; Ofsted 2005b, 2005c).

Some foundation subjects remain beleaguered and at the deeper level it can even be argued that Geography has suffered, perhaps more than most, from the 'curriculum strait-jacket' and the government's continued approach of pigeon-holing knowledge, skills and understanding into traditional subject areas. Cross-curricular teaching has been rather dominated by the confused and confusing 'need' to attach Literacy and Numeracy to other subjects within the curriculum. Added to this is the perspective of a recent survey conducted by the Geographical Association into initial teacher education. This survey evidences a decrease in both the number of hours devoted to geography and the number of students being trained as primary geography subject specialists (Geographical Association Teacher Education Working Group 2004).

Her Majesty's Chief Inspector of Schools has repeatedly reported on the potential of geography's offering, pointing to the subject's role in developing practical and analytical skills (Ofsted 2002) and citing the range of major world issues that provide us with the geography of today (Bell 2005; Ofsted 2004). However, the focus of all Ofsted primary geography reports in recent years has been ongoing failings in teaching, curriculum leadership and management in the subject. The Ofsted Subject Report of 2003/04 uncompromisingly started with the statement that geography provision was, by then, weaker than in any other National Curriculum subject – only 33 per cent of overall provision was good, very good or excellent (Ofsted 2005a). The Chief Inspector is clear about the challenge facing the geography community, 'this challenge is for the hearts and minds of future generations of pupils and to make geography more useful, more relevant and more interesting.' (Bell 2005: 5). Important though it is to contextualise Ofsted's view as one that is particularly focused on teaching rather than on learning (Catling 2004b), the fact that inspectors continue to see little geography being taught during their inspections can be blamed on teachers' perception of the subject as conceptual, less specific and more skills-based (Bell 2005) and can probably be blamed on a real anxiety about geography in primary teachers' minds.

One 'unwritten rule' of geographical teaching and learning, that activity in the field should be a central component of a robust geography curriculum, has suffered some significant challenge from certain quarters in recent years. A massive body of research work explores the importance and complexity of direct experience in children's learning about place (Matthews 1992), and therefore the assumed relevance of fieldwork (Chambers 1995), but a battery of reasons for avoiding taking children beyond the classroom door have combined to further impact on creative geographical learning for many children. Squeeze on curri-culum time, lack of expertise among primary subject leaders, anxieties held by teachers, head teachers, governing bodies and parents – as well as negative media hype – have all contributed to pressure on one of the most obvious aspects of a creative, relevant and fun geographical education. There is clear evidence that fieldwork in primary schools is 'underdeveloped', that use of the outdoor environment in the Foundation Stage tends to focus narrowly on 'the natural world' and that use of the local environment is particularly poor in Key Stage 2 (Ofsted 2005c).

Looking to the future – innovation and personalisation

If there is a new dawn, then it is heralded by Primary National Strategy references (DfES 2003) and Ofsted's reporting that the best primary schools combine high standards with a broad and rich curriculum. The Strategy advocates schools and their teaching staff taking ownership of the curriculum and being creative and innovative in how they teach. The implication, seemingly, is a central desire to see the 'strait-jacket' loosened with teachers realising freedoms in timetable design and curriculum content, framed by a renewed focus on 'Excellence and Enjoyment'. Interviewed in 1995 Ted Wragg suggested, 'There's not much enjoyment in *Excellence and Enjoyment* at the moment . . . If you do a word search on it, there's not an awful lot of enjoyment there.' (Wragg, T., interviewed in Wilson, A. (1995), p. 185). Perhaps there is now new hope that the profession is prepared to inject the required 'enjoyment' to make the document live up to its title.

Further hope is offered by the QCA's increasing focus on 'futures thinking' and innovation within subjects. Meaningful debate has involved the wider geographical teaching community and subject associations. Discussions have centred on the structure and effectiveness of the geography curriculum, assessment processes and making assessment evidence work, and on the professional development of teachers (Geographical Association 2005). The QCA's 'five forces for change' – changes in society and the nature of work, the impact of technology, new understanding about learning, the need for greater personalisation of the curriculum and scope for innovation and the increasingly international dimension to life and work – seem particularly relevant to geography's futures debate (QCA 2005a, 2005b). Following 'summits' with curriculum representatives from the geography community during 2005 the QCA recommended eight challenges for the subject (QCA 2005a) listed under the question 'what do we need to do?':

- move towards an aims-based curriculum;
- develop a more flexible curriculum;
- promote the importance of geography;
- enhance understanding of learning and progression in geography;
- strengthen support for teachers;
- develop a sound conceptual and skill-based framework;
- improve links with higher education;
- improve links between subjects.

At the time of writing we wait for further outcomes from the QCA 'Futures' 'summits' and associated working and, of course, the acid test will be how such discussion and pondering will ultimately impact on change in schools and pupil learning.

What is clear is that we are getting a better understanding of the evidence that Ofsted and other sources are providing on good geographical learning and teaching. Catling (2004a) lists good and better teachers of primary geography as:

- clear about the geographical intentions of units of work and lessons;
- using a variety of creative and engaging teaching methods and activities;
- able to differentiate tasks while ensuring suitable challenge;
- making use of appropriate vocabulary;
- employing demanding questioning techniques;
- involving pupils in debate;
- supporting work with effective resources; and
- using formative assessment proactively to respond to pupils' needs in lessons.

This list emphasises the central role of the teacher as underpinning a learner-centred focus whereby the teacher is seen as having 'responsibilities' in providing effective early years and primary geographical education. Catling (2003) suggests that these responsibilities should include:

- drawing on the geographical experiences of children, taking the curriculum from the child and building it for the child;

- working with and from children's inquisitiveness about the environment and people;

- ensuring creativity and rigour in task structure, approach and challenge;

- the imaginative and disciplined use of a variety of active learning-teaching strategies;

- recognising and appreciating what is learned from geographical studies with the children;

- providing access to resources, locally/globally, in the variety of forms available, from the text- and article-based to the visual, virtual and human, from local to global sources; and

- recognising and evaluating the value, learning and limitations of the study undertaken with the children.

Lack of confidence of non-specialist teachers exaggerated further by a shortage of capable geography subject leaders has tended to mean a default reliance on the QCA schemes of work for geography rather than a recognition of responsibilities such as those above.

While Ofsted recognises that schemes of work have sometimes been adapted to meet the specific requirements of the school and the resources available, they go on to caution that in many schools the schemes have resulted in a disjointed, content-based curriculum resultant of failures to adapt them sufficiently to local circumstances. In addition they state that there is often a lack of rationale for unit selection and a lack of progression in the teaching of multiple units (Ofsted 2005a). The Geographical Association's *Primary Geography Handbook* encourages the subject leader to answer the question 'If you use the QCA units, to what extent do you modify and adapt them to match local needs and resources?' (Foley 2004: 351) . . . labelling it as a key Ofsted issue.

Encouragement to work in a more cross-curricular way, to develop new approaches to timetabling and to be more innovative and prepared to embrace approaches to personalise the curriculum must be used to help liberate teachers from over-reliance on unadapted units in contexts lacking rationale.

Taking control of learning and the curriculum

To those of us who care for the state of geographical and environmental education in the early years and primary phase it seems that the fuel of fascinating, topical and real geographical issues is more than in place. The media coverage of local, national and global issues is now outstanding at catching young children's attention and imagination. The oxygen of permitting circumstances is now being pumped back into nursery and primary settings as QCA signals revised ways of engaging with curriculum design in schools, as subject advocates like the Geographical Association join the QCA in providing quality, targeted subject support, resources, interpretation and training. All that is now needed is a new spark to ignite this mix.

Such a spark may be provided by the timing of the publication of the Geographical Association's *Primary Geography Handbook* (Scoffham 2004), the 'futures thinking' at the QCA and, possibly, by a new focus within the media and education sectors on 'really big issues'. The tsunami of December 2004, the run-up to the Gleneagles G8 Summit – with perspectives on Africa and environmental sustainability – Hurricanes Katrina and Rita and their aftermath, and the South Asia earthquake are examples of issues that genuinely engage the minds of the young and of their teachers. The 'spark' has to include effective delivery of interpretation of the geography within these issues such that it can be utilised in new personalised and innovative curricula.

If there is a new geographical oxygen then it is necessary that those who call for it understand a little more about how children learn good geography. Because the subject inevitably includes learning about the complex and the geographically distant, the power balance in determining curriculum coverage at primary level has tended to reside with adults who see themselves as 'owning' this knowledge. If we question the purpose of a geographical education we can begin to invest a greater belief in children's own geographies. Each child has a unique relationship with the world (Palmer 1994) and a geography structured around children's own enquiries – and that genuinely explores their own 'personal geographies' (Catling 2003) – is far more likely to provide the needed spark. It can be argued that there is a need for those with responsibility for children's learning in geography to recognise that the world in which the child lives can be very different from the world of the adult and some authors advocate a curriculum more mindful of the lessons of Cultural Geography and Citizenship to highlight the 'people' in geography (Hoodless *et al.* 2003).

Those who educate teachers, those who provide them with subject leadership and those who lead on curriculum development have a new encouragement to recraft the geographical experiences of pupils. There may be an opportunity to build the curriculum more around children as active participants (Catling 2003; Chambers 1995) and it is suggested that a re-examination of cross-curricular opportunities and a new look at the overall structure of the curriculum will allow this.

Geography as a statutory subject

There has been a long-lived debate around geography's position as a subject in its own right. In the period before we heard that geography was to be a National Curriculum subject David Mills advocated a subject approach in a time when geographical learning was mainly taught through combined study frameworks:

The main advantage of teaching geography as a separate subject is that it will be more likely to have properly considered schemes of work and may well also have a trained geographer either to teach many parts of the syllabus or at least to be available to give help and assistance to teachers who might not have had a geographical background.

(Mills 1988: 238)

Shortly after the inception of the National Curriculum for Geography Bill Marsden suggested that, 'there is no built-in incompatibility between good primary practice and good subject practice, in this case related to geography' (Marsden 1994: 1). Geography is now established as a subject in its own right although, rather ironically, the very point that Mills raised regarding the need for trained geographers, at least as subject leaders, is now a major issue raised by the Chief Inspector (Ofsted 2005a) and one of the biggest challenges facing primary geography.

Recent years have seen a succession of National Curriculum Orders placing simple emphasis on locality studies and certain geographical themes. The word 'locality' has been the basis for whole lectures within teacher education courses and the gradual process of moving the Statutory Orders to the present situation where there is a 'breadth of study' requiring locality study has been a long one. The present Orders define 'locality' for us:

The 'locality' of the school is its immediate vicinity, including school buildings and grounds and the surrounding area within easy access. The contrasting locality should be an area of similar size.

(DFEE/QCA 1999: 17)

Similarly, the Orders include specific themes in Key Stage 2 – one based around water and its effects on people and places including physical processes, one around settlements and changing land use, and one around an environmental issue and sustainable management of the environment.

Although there has been a 'relaxation' of the earlier content-heavy versions of the Orders (DES 1991; DfE 1995) which, each time, reduced the numbers of localities and themes to be covered, it can be argued that between 1991 and 1999 there was a significant relative reduction in preparedness of non-specialist teachers to acquaint themselves with the potential of the curriculum. Almost certainly this was partly due to anxiety by non-specialist class teachers who saw the locality and thematic expectations as demanding – not least with respect to finding the right resources. This period coincided with the launch of the National Strategies and the sum damage to creative planning and teaching of geography, and the timetable provided for it in primary schools was palpable.

Many non-specialist teachers may simply have found the idea of researching, resourcing and teaching about places, according to the National Curriculum's definition of locality, as too daunting. The large numbers of orders for locality packs and scheme of work resources on Chembakolli (Action Aid 1991), St Lucia (Bunce *et al*, 1992), Godstone (Walker and Wetton 1995) and Llandudno (QCA 1998) and so many more may, with hindsight, make testament to this.

The places, themes and skills construction that has underpinned the geography orders has stood the test of time, albeit with improvements to the setting of 'knowledge, skills and understanding' against a 'breadth of study' component in the most recent version. Also proving its longevity is the notion of running key geographical questions through geographical studies. Under 'Knowledge and Understanding of Places', children are encouraged to enquire into the places they learn about with five key questions framed in Key Stage 1 and seven in Key Stage 2. These questions owe their origin to an article by Michael Storm in an early *Primary Geographer* magazine (Storm 1989) but have been developed many times since. The Geographical Association's *Primary Geography Handbook* suggests 11 questions that might aid effective enquiry for environmental observation (Catling 2004a).

There is an identifiable progression from the Foundation Stage to Key Stage 2, a progression based on expanding outwards from the immediate and local, from children's direct experience to indirect experience and from the personal to the abstract. Blyth and Krause (1995) famously developed this approach into notions of 'Little Geography' and 'Big Geography' and, in the *Handbook*, Catling has now helped by interpreting the National Curriculum in terms of a progression in geographical learning. He suggests that in the Foundation Stage children are 'Encountering Geography', that Years 1 and 2 are about 'Geographical Awareness', Years 3 and 4 about 'Geographical Engagement' and that in Years 5 and 6 pupils should experience 'Geographical Involvement' (Catling 2004a).

Moving forward

Clearly, there is work to be done in driving primary and early years geography forward. Catling (2003, 2004b) repeatedly points to the good news about the subject and that in some schools good and excellent geography can be identified.

In setting the course for the following chapters, a gathering context of permitting circumstances has been described. It has been argued that massively improving subject support from organisations such as the Geographical Association – exemplified by the new *Handbook* – along with a renewed vigour in interpreting the provisions of the Primary National Strategy and a stimulating QCA 'futures' debate are providing a new 'spark'.

It is hoped that the discussion, reflection and case studies that follow will help provide additional stimulus to those keen to see their pupils learn in a creative, critical, meaningful and emotionally intelligent way about the world, their place in it and the responsibilities that they and others have towards its future.

References

Action Aid (1991) *Chembakolli: A Village in India*. London: Action Aid.

Bale, J. (1987) *Geography in the Primary School*. London: Routledge & Kegan Paul.

Bell, D. (2005) 'The value and importance of geography', *Primary Geographer*, **56**, 4–5.

Blades, M. and Spencer, C. (1986) 'Map use by young children', *Geography*, **71** (1), 47–52.

Blaut, J. and Stea, D. (1974) 'Mapping at the age of three', *Journal of Geography*, **73**, 5–9.

Blow, D. (2004) 'Geography: inclusion and special needs', in Scoffham, S. (ed.) *Primary Geography Handbook*. Sheffield: Geographical Association, pp. 322–33.

Blyth, A. and Krause, J. (1995) *Primary Geography: A Developmental Approach*. London: Hodder & Stoughton.

Bunce, V., Foley, J., Morgan, W. and Scobie, S. (1992) *Focus on Castries, St Lucia*. Sheffield: Geographical Association/Sutton: Worldaware.

Carter, R. (1998) *Handbook of Primary Geography*. Sheffield: Geographical Association.

Catling, S. (2003) 'Curriculum contested: primary geography and social justice', *Geography*, **88** (3), 164–210.

Catling, S. (2004a) 'Understanding and developing primary geography', in Scoffham, S. (ed.) *Primary Geography Handbook*. Sheffield: Geographical Association, pp. 75–91.

Catling, S. (2004b) 'On close inspection', *Primary Geographer*, **55**, 34–6.

Chambers, W. (1995) *Awareness into Action: Environmental Education in the Primary Classroom*. Sheffield: Geographical Association.

DES (1991) *Geography in the National Curriculum (England)*. London: HMSO.

DFE (1995) *Geography in the National Curriculum*. London: HMSO.

DfEE/QCA (1999) *The National Curriculum for England: Geography*. London: DfEE/QCA.

DfEE/QCA (2000) *Curriculum Guidance for the Foundation Stage*. London: DfEE/QCA.

DfES (2003) *Excellence and Enjoyment: A Strategy for Primary Schools*. London: DfES.

Dinkele, G. (2004) 'Geographical enquiries and investigations', in Scoffham, S. (ed.) *Primary Geography Handbook*. Sheffield: Geographical Association, pp. 94–103.

Foley, M. (2004) 'The inspection process', in Scoffham, S. (ed.) *Primary Geography Handbook*. Sheffield: Geographical Association, pp. 349–57.

Geographical Association (2005) *The Power and Future of Geography in Schools* (www.geography.org.uk/news/powerofgeography/articles) (online discussion paper). Sheffield: Geographical Association.

Geographical Association Teacher Education Working Group (2004) 'The state of primary geography in ITE', *Primary Geographer*, **53**, 43.

Gould, P. and White, R. (1974) *Mental Maps*. Harmondsworth: Penguin.

Hart, R. (1979) *Children's Experience of Place*. New York: Irvington.

Hoodless, P., Bermingham, S., McCreery, E. and Bowen, P. (2003) *Teaching Humanities in Primary Schools*. Exeter: Learning Matters.

Marsden, B. (1994) 'Places and peoples: continuity and change in primary geography', in Marsden, B. and Hughes, J. *Primary School Geography*. London: David Fulton Publishers, pp. 1–8.

Martin, F. (1995) *Teaching Early Years Geography*. Cambridge: Chris Kington Publishing.

Martin, F. and Owens, P. (2004) 'Young children making sense of their place in the world', in Scoffham, S. (ed.) *Primary Geography Handbook*. Sheffield: Geographical Association, pp. 62–73.

Matthews, M. (1992) *Making Sense of Place: Children's Understanding of Large-Scale Environments*. Hemel Hempstead: Harvester Wheatsheaf.

Mills, D. (1988) 'The teaching of geography as a separate subject', in Mills, D. (ed.) *Geographical Work in Primary and Middle Schools*. Sheffield: Geographical Association.

Ofsted (2002) *Geography in Primary Schools: Ofsted Subject Reports 2001/02*. London: Ofsted.

Ofsted (2004) *News Release 115*, 24 November. London: Ofsted.

Ofsted (2005a) *Geography in Primary Schools: Ofsted Subject Reports 2003/04*. London: Ofsted.

Ofsted (2005b) *News Release 10*, 2 February. London: Ofsted.

Ofsted (2005c) *Annual Report of Her Majesty's Chief Inspector of Schools 2004/05*. London: Ofsted.

Palmer, J. (1994) *Geography in the Early Years*. London: Routledge.

Pattison, W. (1964) 'The four traditions of geography', *Journal of Geography*, **63**, 211–16.

Qualifications and Curriculum Authority (1998) *Unit 13: A Contrasting UK Locality – Llandudno*. London: QCA.

Qualifications and Curriculum Authority (2005a) *A Curriculum for the Future: Subjects Consider the Challenge*. London: QCA.

Qualifications and Curriculum Authority (2005b) 'Futures: meeting the challenge', *Geography Update*, Spring, 16.

Richardson, P. (2004a) 'Planning the geography curriculum', in Scoffham, S. (ed.) *Primary Geography Handbook*. Sheffield: Geographical Association, pp. 302–11.

Richardson, P. (2004b) 'Fieldwork', in Scoffham, S. (ed.) *Primary Geography Handbook*. Sheffield: Geographical Association, pp. 134–47.

Scoffham, S. (ed.) (2004) *Primary Geography Handbook*. Sheffield: Geographical Association.

Storm, M. (1989) 'The five basic questions for primary geography', *Primary Geographer*, **2**, 4.

Tanner, J. (2004) 'Geography and the emotions', in Scoffham, S. (ed.) *Primary Geography Handbook*. Sheffield: Geographical Association, pp. 34–47.

Walker, G. and Wetton, S. (1995) *Discover Godstone*. Coalville: Wildgoose.

Wiegand, P. (1992) *Places in the Primary School*. London: Falmer Press.

Wiegand, P. (1993) *Children and Primary Geography*. London: Cassell.

Wilson, A. (ed.) (1995) *Creativity in Primary Education*. Exeter: Learning Matters.

Young, M. (2004) 'Geography and the global dimension', in Scoffham, S. (ed.) *Primary Geography Handbook*. Sheffield: Geographical Association, pp. 216–29.

Planning and assessment

Are there different types of geographical enquiry?

Chris Rowley

There are grounds for suspicion that the kind of environmental education supported by current policy may be largely cosmetic when measured against the depth and complexity of the issues at stake.

(Bonnett 2004)

BONNETT'S TIMELY BOOK, *Retrieving Nature: Education for a Post-Humanist Age*, raises fundamental questions about the nature of education, particularly environmental education, today. Since geography in the primary curriculum often lies at the heart of children's school-based experience of environmental issues (particularly through the sustainable development aspect of its programme of study), it is important that we ask fundamental questions about that experience. This chapter considers some of those questions, and the options that we need to investigate in selecting types of geographical enquiry. Currently variants of deductive enquiry form the basis of much teaching in primary geography. While recognising that 'rational' thinking is likely to provide the ultimate solution to human/environment problems, it is here argued that an understanding of, and a creative response to, that rationality will only come through enquiries which develop a sense of awe and wonder, a background of aesthetic awareness and a framework of ethical consideration. Geography has the potential to identify these links if it can ensure that there are different types of enquiry developing different 'ways' of knowing.

While an enquiry approach to learning has been widely identified as one of the most desirable learning processes, it is almost certainly one of the most difficult to put into practice. Teachers are expected to do so much: enthuse, achieve standards, teach skills, encourage thinking, monitor, assess and teach key facts in a world where certainty is rapidly replaced by doubt. How, at the same time, can teachers encourage enquiry approaches driven by children's own curiosity? What are the triggers from which enquiry develops? Can an enquiry be reflective and involve group work? Should enquiry begin to challenge some of the assumptions by which we lead our lives? This chapter will attempt to answer some of these questions.

The National Curriculum has focused our attention on defining the nature of enquiry in each subject, though the differences have not always been clear because there is so much overlap between subjects. Geographical enquiry relies upon a range of skills and concepts which, used together, help us to understand the relationship between people and their environment. Identifying those skills and concepts which specifically contribute to this has never been easy, partly because of the tendency of geographers themselves to separate out human and physical geography. The key objectives of geographical enquiry make it particularly well placed as a unifying subject in primary schools. Geography has always aimed to integrate knowledge of the human and the physical world. We do not do the subject justice if we separate those areas. Since enquiry in the classroom is widely recognised as the most desirable and fundamental means of developing geographical understanding, it is surprising to find so few references to approaches to enquiry at Key Stage 2.

Finding how we can encourage children to link their own experiences to the 'bigger questions' is one aim of this chapter. Can eight-year-olds link their experience of their place to understanding 'places' in general? Can children translate their own experience of crossing the road to bigger questions relating to our reliance upon cars?

Why geographical enquiry?

Geographical enquiry has a rich background of research and implementation through a range of projects and initiatives since the mid-1960s at Key Stage 3, particularly in schools council projects. (See the excellent summary in Roberts 2003, Chap. 1.) There has been less variety of innovation at Key Stages 1 and 2.

Geographical enquiry is important for the following reasons:

1 Geographical enquiry influences WHAT we learn (THE CONTENT).

2 Geographical enquiry influences HOW we learn (THE PROCESS).

3 Geographical enquiry can develop the interdisciplinary skills and understandings that are essential outcomes for future societies (THE OUTCOMES).

If these three constitute enquiry then it is clear that there is an assumed link between 'knowing' in terms of what and how, and in acting through the outcomes. Experience suggests, however, that these are only tenuously linked in our society. Many people 'know' sufficient regarding, say, global climate change, but very few act upon that or accept any personal responsibility for it.

Geographical enquiry also searches for questions, but these easily become descriptive questions. Such questions are important, but they tend to be unreflective and need to be linked to the bigger questions that underlie them if we are to encourage deeper thinking. These bigger questions are reliant upon a recognition of a set of concepts. Choosing stimuli for enquiry where the concepts are embedded will help the development of the bigger questions. (Examples of these 'bigger' questions can be seen in the examples later in this chapter.)

Characteristics of geographical enquiry

Geographical enquiry develops from questions and requires a growing ability to:

- relate diverse sources of geographical information (in primary schools this might mean using photographs alongside maps and managing to question and make judgements based on both)
- make use of a set of spatial skills (this includes a range of map interpretation skills such as recognising perspective, scale and key symbols)
- relate ideas to specific geographical aspects of concepts (these include community, interdependence, location, diversity, pattern; process and environmental change)
- account for both factual and value-based dimensions together.

At Key Stage 3 recent authors, for example Roberts (2003) and Taylor (2004), have looked in depth at alternative ways of managing classroom enquiry. Roberts (2003: 139) contrasts geographical enquiry and historical enquiry, referring to Riley (1999) who found history teachers asking much more specific questions in order to capture interest and identify an aspect of historical thinking. We need to be sure that geographical enquiry has a rigour and a clear purpose related to the overall objective of geography. How is geographical enquiry different from enquiry in other subjects? Should it be? Is geography wise in maintaining its more open approach to enquiry compared with history?

Geographical enquiry now

Storm (1989) proposed five key questions which could be used as a stimulus for geographical enquiry. These are sometimes called 'key' questions in the literature of geographical education.

1 What is this place like?
2 Why is it like that?
3 How is this place connected to other places?
4 How is this place changing?
5 What would it feel like to live in this place?

These questions are widely accepted as fundamental components of geographical investigation at Key Stages 1 and 2. In addition to being immensely useful in helping teachers focus their geography, they have many more questions embedded in them and, used well, they have performed an important service in the development of geographical work in the primary school.

It may be, however, that their usefulness in the early development of the National Curriculum in Geography should now be reassessed. New and more varied ways of stimulating geographical enquiry need to be considered in order to meet the demands that now face teachers in implementing geography in an environment where creativity, inclusion and enjoyment have been given a new status in the subject's development. The five key questions still help in clarifying certain aspects of geographical investigation. Unfortunately though, they have been widely misunderstood in the process of transferring them to the classroom environment. Storm himself recognised the hazards inherent in the questions, but scant regard has been paid to these since his original article appeared in 1989. These included the hazard of environmental determinism (presenting lifestyles as entirely determined by physical environment), arising from the question 'why is this place like this?' There is a danger of encouraging empathy from an inadequate information base (arising from the question 'what would it feel like to live in this place?'). What he didn't envisage in that article was that these questions would so easily be confused with the purpose or the trigger of the enquiry.

The use of these key questions in the QCA schemes has not helped. There appears to be some confusion in their use as a planning tool, in which the teacher plans a scheme around a key question approach, and their use as a starting point for children's own enquiry. Children's questions are frequently lost by the rigidity of learning outcomes that the key questions approach can easily propagate. Conceptual understanding in geography has been one of the prime losers, partly because the questions lend themselves easily to descriptive responses which miss the underlying concepts. This contrasts with much material on enquiry produced for Key Stage 3 (Roberts 2003; Taylor 2004: 68, 65–6) for example. They emphasise the need for an approach in which 'interesting questions' drive the enquiry, and offers strategies to develop these questions.

Frameworks for geographical enquiry

The deductive enquiry framework

Searches on educational databases or indeed on more general internet sites reveal little variation in the models of enquiry proposed for classroom use. The key questions have been, rightly or wrongly, associated with an essentially deductive model of enquiry, one which bases its approach on logic. Essentially primary geography most often uses a 'one size fits all' mode of enquiry which involves raising questions; collecting and recording information; processing and analysing that data; sharing the outcomes; evaluating.

This essentially deductive model of enquiry is fine for many geographical investigations. This is particularly the case with those which are based essentially on logical understanding of the environment (typical of physical geography but also applicable in understanding basic human patterns at an elementary level). It seems strange that primary geographical enquiry has taken the deductive enquiry route when there is such a rich background of values enquiry in geography. If one of the objectives of geographical education is to challenge children's assumptions about the world, then values enquiry has to be a central component of that. Is processing data really a useful approach to enquiring into values? 'More intimate, intuitive, often sensuous and non-logical encounters with things must be admitted' (Bonnett 2004: 139).

Other frameworks of enquiry

Many areas of geography would benefit from an approach to enquiry which starts from values and ideas rather than from information collection; an approach where thinking and talking together replaces gathering and garnering information as the starting point (see, for example, Mackintosh 2005). It is clear that there are different 'ways of knowing' which are derived from different ways of enquiring. Aesthetic appreciation, ethical judgement and a sense of wonder are all equally important aspects of enquiry and are also essential in learning to be aware of, and prepare for, change in a complex human/physical environment. Sterling (2001) takes this a stage further by suggesting that learning itself should be seen as, 'change, a process in which we constantly re-visit and challenge ideas which are generally taken for granted'.

Roberts (2003: 44–6) identifies a framework for enquiry learning at Key Stage 3 which essentially uses the deductive method even in values enquiries. In other words, the four stages of questioning, data collection, analysis (making sense) and reflection (evaluation) are used. That approach differs from those used in many of the following examples. Here a framework is used which starts from a concept and a skill but then uses verbal enquiries which do not always follow the deductive route. These examples each identify a key concept and a skill. Good geographical enquiry is built upon the ability to use these cumulatively in order to understand the relationship between people and environment. Each example tries to demonstrate how openness is maintained alongside direction through teacher intervention. The real enquiry might only begin with the questions raised for further enquiry at the bottom of each framed example and in many cases at Key Stages 1 and 2 this will be a verbal enquiry. Some examples are enquiries which encourage development of ideas without data. Other examples retain a more scientific approach to enquiry in which data is collected and analysed. Many ethical and aesthetic enquiries involve short exercises to focus thinking and reasoning around specific concepts.

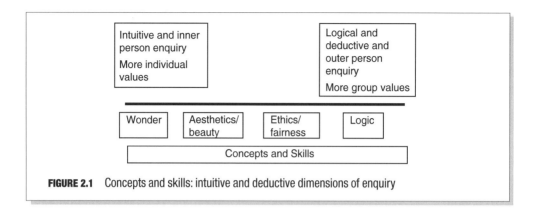

FIGURE 2.1   Concepts and skills: intuitive and deductive dimensions of enquiry

Five considerations before planning a sequence of enquiry lessons

The examples used in the following sections attempt to offer a range of approaches to enquiry encouraging questions around concepts, developing specific skills, while at the same time linking to the National Curriculum. Table 2.1 shows how these examples relate.

TABLE 2.1   Summary of different enquiries used to illustrate this chapter

Example number	Year group	Relationship to key questions approach	Key concept	Key skill	National Curriculum link
Figure 2.2	5	Links to all the key questions	Boundaries	Description	Identify and explain what places are like
Figure 2.3	3	What would it feel like to live in this place?	Perceptions of place	Choosing appropriate examples	Explain why places are like they are
Figure 2.4	6	How is this place changing?	Preferences	Making choices	Recognise how people can improve the environment and damage it
Figure 2.5	6	How is this place changing?	Change	Classifying	Recognise change in the environment
Figure 2.6	5	What is this place like?	Pattern	Recognising differences	Recognise and explain patterns made by physical and human environmental features
Figure 2.7	5	What is this place like?	Wilderness	Making distinctions	Identify and describe what places are like

Children's geographies and enquiry learning

Probably the most significant development in our understanding of geographical learning in the last 15 years has been the increasing recognition of the importance of the geographies that children themselves bring to the classroom. The most comprehensive and wide-ranging account of the background to this approach is almost certainly that of Catling in his professorial address at Oxford Brookes University in 2003. The paper, published in *Geography*, July 2003, ranges widely across the research which has identified geographies that influence children's development. His analysis of the implications of this for the primary curriculum should be essential reading for all interested in the role and the future of primary school geography. Applying the findings to enquiry geography, Catling proposes a '3 E's' approach to initiating children into an enquiry approach.

- Enabling Enquiry: in which the teacher acts as enabler, drawing and focusing on the children's own questions and drawing on their sense of exploration and inquisitiveness.

- Enhancing Enquiry: in which the teacher challenges children's questions to focus them consistently on matters of geographical relevance in relation to which children take greater responsibility for refining their enquiry through the selection of approaches and methods.

- Empowering Enquiry: in which children take greater responsibility for refining the enquiry, through the selection of approaches and methods.

In identifying these approaches Catling draws attention to the way in which geographical enquiry in this model reflects the ideals of a philosophical exploration, characterised in a 'community of enquiry', a whole-class, open enquiry, in which questions are chosen by the children. Certainly a 'community of enquiry' using this definition offers real possibilities in geographical education, not least because values are so deeply embedded in both geographical issues and in children's own geographies. A community of enquiry is centred around talk, in which children choose the central question democratically and the teacher facilitates the discussion by asking what are known as 'Socratic' questions ('How would you know if that is true?'; 'Can you say why you think that?' are examples of such questions). More information on this approach can be found at the website of SAPERE (The Society to Advance Philosophical Enquiry and Reflection in Education) at www.sapere.net. Here the term is developed to become a 'philosophical community of enquiry'.

While the analysis helps in moving our thinking forward it ignores some very real issues in the practice of this type of enquiry. Among the questions the approach raises are, for example, can this approach offer the rigour of scientific enquiry? How does the teacher on the one hand encourage open questioning and on the other focus that questioning? By identifying a key skill and a concept can the open nature of the enquiry be lost? Considerable development can be seen in the Geographical Association's 'Valuing Places' project (www.geography.org.uk/valuingplaces).

The geographies that children bring to the classroom can also be more directly developed through children's personal maps. Roberts (2003: 164–78) pays particular attention to personal geographies at Key Stage 3, identifying how personal experience can be incorporated into much geographical work. Some of these approaches also apply to Key Stages 1 and 2, particularly 'affective mapping'. (The continuing professional development units, such as 'messy maps', on the Geographical Association's valuing places website, encourage children to bring their own understanding of places to their maps.)

Year 5
Key concept: Boundaries
Skill: Description
Trigger for enquiry: A visit to some nearby wasteland or park with which children are familiar
National Curriculum link: Identify and explain what places are like

Activity
1. Do a map memory exercise (see bottom of opposite panel for an explanation).
2. Draw a map of the school showing where you can go and where you can't go. Children can also mark feelings on the map with suitable symbols.
3. Before visiting the park or wasteland find it on Google Earth (free download). As you zoom in on the location ask children to identify boundaries that they recognise. Are there places that they can and can't go? Are some boundaries invisible?

Exercise: On the visit identify features that you did and did not see on Google Earth. Why do some boundaries seem to show up but not others? Are there boundaries in their lives that are or are not on the Google Earth image? One question is chosen for a whole-class discussion in which children's experiences of the place are developed.

The concept of boundaries
Geography is fundamentally about places and to understand places we need to know the limits of that place. When we look at a map or an air photograph we are only able to analyse it if we ask why certain patterns emerge. Google Earth is an excellent free web-based resource for identifying boundaries and patterns at a variety of scales depending on how far you zoom in. Children's lives are governed by boundaries of where they can and where they can't go, where they feel safe or unsafe. Any good geographical enquiry should encourage questions about why that is the case.

The skill of describing
Description should not always be downgraded to a low-level skill. An ability to describe what we see is crucial to all geographical enquiry. Margaret Roberts (2003, Chap. 9: 112–27) gives a number of exercises to develop description skills through enquiry in geography at KS3 (Chinese whispers, Venn diagrams, writing frames, identifying links, etc.). Many of these are equally used at KS2. In this lesson a map memory exercise increases the powers of description. A map of the place being investigated is centrally placed and covered up. Each group of children sends one at a time to have 15 seconds observation time before returning to the desk and helping the others in their group reconstruct the map.

Why are there boundaries?

FIGURE 2.2 Focus on children's geographies

Another element of children's geographies is their perception of place, both places they know and places that they do not know. It is now common practice to gather perceptions prior to studying a distant place. The evidence that we will be using is likely to be secondary, and as a result drama could be used to encourage children to relate their real perceptions, rather than those which may be what they believe are expected (see Chapter 5 for an example.) Bridge (2005) proposes that a child's experience is extended by geographical studies in four key ways: personal, social, intellectual and emotional. It follows that any study of a distant place needs to offer opportunities to engage with the material at these levels.

Year 3
Key concept: Perceptions of place
Skill: Choosing appropriate examples
Trigger for enquiry: Pictures of Mexico
National Curriculum link: Explain why places are like they are

Activity: After looking at the photographs, discuss the images that we have of Mexico. Cacti, big hats, palm trees, etc.

Exercise: Devise a group tableau (still life picture) to show to others a place which has some features, people or events which describe it simply. Use questions like the ones below, or devise your own, which help to find out what sort of place it is.

Is it a working place or a relaxing place?
Is it a natural place or a man-made place?
Is it a changing place?
Is it a big place or a small place? Outdoors or indoors?

In discussing the tableau we may need to draw attention to the counter examples of places, e.g. A favourite garden might be both a relaxing place and a working place.

Questions raised for further enquiry:
How else do we know about places?

What makes us care for places?

Do we always like hot places?

The concept of perception
How we perceive a place is partly governed by how places are represented to us. Both Roberts (2003) and Taylor (2004) recognise the importance of how places are represented to us for geographical enquiry. Techniques often used to develop enquiries in this area include contrasting images, marketing places, belonging in places, etc. In this example, pitched at KS2, children create a group 'tableau' or still life picture which describes the place. Each child will represent someone doing something in that place. When the group presents its still life to the class the teacher and children can 'visit' the tableau, asking questions in trying to identify what is being represented.

The skill of choosing examples and counter examples
The ability to give examples to prove a point and counter examples to disprove is of great importance in beginning to know how to reason. While primary-aged children often have difficulty giving reasons they are often good at giving examples. In this case children are asked to give examples of places which fulfil certain criteria, e.g. places which we think are hot; places where we think people are poor. There will always be counter examples to suggest these places are not like that.

FIGURE 2.3 Focus on perceptions of place

Stimulating children's questions

Most models of enquiry learning encourage children to ask what are seen as specific geographical questions. There is a danger here that we miss opportunities by narrowing children's creativity into a restricted perception of what geography is. The biggest challenge in the approaches to enquiry proposed in this chapter is the need for the teacher to recognise the geography often embedded in 'big' questions which may on the surface not be purely geographical. The following example (Figure 2.4) illustrates children asking big difficult questions which appear to come from deep-rooted concerns rather than from a quick analysis of the information given. These questions can be handled through class discussion and are just as important in enquiry as the more logically-driven questions that we are familiar with. In this instance the question had to be broken down into what we could discuss for the enquiry to progress. An enquiry into responsibility developed.

Conceptual understanding in geography

The work of Leat (2000) and Higgins and Baumfield (2001) has had much influence on how geographical education is seen. Of all their work, the recognition of the importance of conceptual understanding is perhaps most important (Leat, in Fisher and Binns 2000). Geography has often suffered from an over-reliance on skills teaching at the expense of conceptual understanding. Any model of enquiry learning must pay proper regard to the concepts that are central to geography and for that reason the planning grid for enquiry offered in this chapter proposes that each lesson or group of lessons identifies a key concept upon which the enquiry questions focus. These concepts are clear in the National Curriculum, but in reality each concept encompasses many others which are required for a full understanding. For example. 'Location' involves understanding boundaries, communication and diversity. The examples in Figures 2.2 to 2.7 include some of these concepts but their close relation to those listed in the National Curriculum make them equally valid as a focus for geographical enquiry. The following example (Figure 2.5) focuses on the concept of change but offers opportunities to develop the enquiry into related concepts.

Most concepts are made up of others and it is often worth asking 'What else would we need to know to begin to understand this concept?' In the example in Figure 2.6 'pattern' is the focus, but different types and frequencies of pattern are explored through artistic work as well as geographical investigation of maps.

The types of thinking that children most frequently use

Deductive enquiry, where we start from lots of examples or data and try to find big ideas and conclusions from that dominate much geographical education. In many cases, however, teachers might use a more inductive enquiry approach, were we start with the

Year 6
Key concept: Preferences
Skill: Making choices
Trigger for enquiry: A set of photographs (a pylon; a mobile phone mast; a motorway; a hydro-electric power station; a wind turbine)
National Curriculum link: Recognise how people can improve the environment and damage it

Activity: Group asked to sort the photographs between those that they would and would not like to have in their backyard.

Exercise: Which of the following do you see as long-term choices and which short-term? Choosing where to live; making friends; saving energy; deciding how to use your spare time? Using solar power instead of coal or gas?

Questions raised for further enquiry: Will this planet always be there? Can humans survive?
One of these questions is chosen democratically by the group and that becomes the focus for a class discussion managed by the teacher.

> Will our planet still be there if we aren't there?

> Why don't we have strict rules for things?

The concept of preferences
Most decisions, even centralised ones, are ultimately driven by preferences rather than logic. When the National Curriculum asks that children recognise how people can improve the environment we must first ensure that there is an understanding of how preferences can be expressed and what effects that expression might or might not have. In this example the lesson is asking children to consider the assumptions that they make when they express a preference. They are 'enquiring' into their own choices.

The skill of making choices
Making choices inevitably involves both personal and group values. Roberts (2003, Chap. 11) discusses strategies such as role-play and hot seating for raising values enquiry. The skill in doing that requires an ability to draw upon a sense of personal responsibility as well as personal preferences. In many ways we could argue that all knowledge we have is irrelevant if we don't learn to make sensible use of it. The question is no longer 'can humans survive?' but more 'do we have a personal responsibility for the consequences of decisions that we make?'. Is damaging the environment by flying any less serious than damaging someone else's environment by smoking? While children may ask the first question (as they did here) it is for the teacher to make the link between that question and personal choice.

FIGURE 2.4 Focus on choice

big ideas and then search for examples to illustrate them. Very often children think inductively and, to the teacher, this can be challenging as the ideas may appear beyond reason. Both inductive and deductive thinking can equally involve reflective thinking.

Taking the concept of wilderness we could think about it from either an 'inductive' or a 'deductive' perspective. For example, inductively thinking about wilderness children might think 'A wilderness is a wild place. I once went to a wild place and there were wild animals there. Wild places have wild animals.' (Inductive thinking has information in the conclusion which was not already in the original premise.) Deductive thinking about wilderness might lead children to think, 'Books and television programmes show wilderness as big open spaces. Often there are no trees and people don't live there. There may be wild animals. That is a wilderness.'

Year 6
Key concept: Change
Skill: Classifying
Trigger for enquiry: Visit to a bird reserve
National Curriculum link: Recognise change in the environment

Activity: Attempt to explain the changes to the number of eider ducks over ten years. (Groups given a list of factors which might explain the changes ranging from local factors, global factors and the methods used to count the birds.) These are sorted by the group.

Exercise: Put a list of other changes into groups, e.g. (1) things that never change, (2) things that change if not watched, (3) things that change only if watched, (4) things that only change if they are not watched: the sun; the sea; the weather; imagination; the light in the fridge; a TV programme; the number of ducks in a pond; a thought.

Questions raised for further enquiry: Would the world be better or worse without changes?

Is there anything on the seashore that stays the same every day?

What are the things in your life that stay the same and which things change?

The concept of change
Change is probably the hardest concept to develop at KS2. Margaret Roberts (2003: 189) devotes a chapter to enquiries into the future at KS3, but evidence suggests this as difficult to develop at KS2. (The use of forecasting, scenarios and prioritising require a sense of time which may not often be present at KS2.) For this reason the example chosen here focuses on relatively short-term change and uses data showing relatively rapid changes in bird populations, together with exercises which focus on children's experience of change. It introduces very different types of factors that might cause change.

The skill of classifying
Classification is a skill widely developed across the curriculum. In geography it is no less important and forms part of a progression of skills from recognising similarity, making distinctions to grouping. In this case study we are using classification skills twice; first in sorting the list of possible factors influencing birds and second in classifying other changes into groups.

FIGURE 2.5 Focus on conceptual understanding of change

These are two very different ways of seeing 'wilderness' and neither is wholly right. They demonstrate two very different ways of finding a definition and have different implications. The first makes a judgement from one example into a general rule. The second makes a rule from a number of examples.

If we are to challenge the assumptions that we live our lives by, then a question such as 'what is wild?' is just as important as 'is this a wild place?'. In the following example the questions about wilderness generated after the activity could lead to an enquiry which is a whole-class discussion.

Areas of understanding and ways of knowing

Philosophers subdivide their understanding of the world into key areas, but have always used a language which can be off-putting to describe those areas (*Epistemology*

Year 5
Key concept: Pattern (i.e. geographical pattern such as the pattern made by a river or the pattern of roads on a map)
Skill: Recognising differences
Trigger for enquiry: After a visit to the coast a class looked at a geology map, an air photograph and a land use map of the area visited
National Curriculum link: Recognise and explain patterns made by physical and human environmental features

Activity: The similarities and differences between these three maps were used to design a textile wall-hanging. Three layers of material sewn together were cut into as a representation of both the patterns and the visit.

Exercise: Which of the following show patterns?

	All the time	Sometimes	Never
The sky			
The sea			
A painting			
A photograph			
A thought			
A day			

Do some patterns look better than other patterns?

The concept of pattern
Identifying a pattern in the landscape is central to enquiry. Geographical questions are often about pattern so offering a stimulus where an initially vague pattern becomes clear is important. Art is an obvious route to follow here. Use the landscape to stimulate a simplification or an abstract representation of the geographical pattern. In the example given the discussion during the creation of the textile wall-hanging was often geographical, drawing upon the visit and the maps for inspiration.

The skill of recognising differences
There are subtle differences between a map and a photograph. Furthermore different maps show different patterns. Central to this example was the difference between the pattern on an air photograph, emphasising vegetation, and the pattern on a map, emphasising roads and settlements.

FIGURE 2.6 Focus on pattern

or ways of knowing; *Metaphysics*, the wonder of what we don't know; *Ethics*, what is right or fair; *Aesthetics*, what is good to appreciate; *Logic*, a means of explaining phenomena). While risking the wrath of philosophers in simplifying the terminology it does seem justifiable to look for a way of applying 'different ways of knowing' to any model of enquiry in geography. One of the strengths of geography as a subject has always been its strong cross-curricular approach. It seems right, therefore, that enquiry in the subject should make use of a wide variety of 'ways of knowing' and not allow itself to be dominated by the logical and more scientific enquiry which is so often

---

Year 5
Key concept: Wilderness
Skill: Making distinctions
Trigger for enquiry: A visit to a stone circle
National Curriculum link: Identify and describe what places are like

Activity: Children hold a mirror to their shoulder and think of one word to describe the picture that they see in the mirror.

Exercise: Children generate a class 'wilderness poem' from the words. They also consider the following in groups: (1) Which of the following could be a wilderness to you? A city street, a garden, a mountain top, the seashore, your thoughts, (2) Rank these in order from most to least wild: the oceans, a waste ground, a park, a field, a beach.

Questions raised for further enquiry:
What is 'wild'?
Is everything wild to someone?

These questions are 'big' in that they are essentially philosophical. However, they also have much relevance to geographical education in that our concept of wilderness drives how we respond to places.

Are there different kinds of wilderness?

The concept of wilderness
We generally use the term wilderness to mean places that are not influenced by people. The reality is that all places are now influenced by people and in many ways a wilderness is a concept of our own minds. Children often want one definition because they have been consistently told to use a dictionary. Sometimes that can be a barrier to learning, standing between us and real understanding because of the necessarily condensed definition. Unfortunately this can often work to prevent change. Many mountain environments in the UK are thought of as wilderness even though they are intensely managed. Perceptions of them as wilderness make change to those landscapes difficult, leading to often unnecessary sheep grazing. For change we need children to 'grow' their definitions by enquiring into their meaning. This is as much a responsibility of geography as any other subject.

The skill of making distinctions
Our lives are dominated by a finely honed set of assumptions which govern much of our behaviour. In geography, for example, we often need to distinguish between real and pretend places; near and distant places, towns and villages, estuary and coast, stream and river. In every case the distinction is not straightforward. A 'distant place' may be a long way away or it may be somewhere geographically near but 'distant' in terms of our feelings or knowledge of it. In this example we are asking children to consider what the distinction is between different meanings of 'wild'. To do this different ways of thinking are needed.

FIGURE 2.7 Focus on types of thinking

---

promoted. We need a model which could give a more rounded approach to geography in the primary school and one which addresses the needs of different abilities, in addition to different learning styles and intelligences, and which also helps to promote reflective thinking. Furthermore, these areas of knowledge need to be related to the geographical questions identified by Storm and so widely used in planning for geographical enquiry. Such a model should offer potential for more depth in answering those questions, and encourage us to identify a wider range of questions within them.

Conclusion

> Unfortunately for the traveller, most objects don't come affixed with a question that will generate the excitement they deserve. There is virtually nothing fixed to them at all, or if there is, it tends to be the wrong thing.
>
> (De Botton 2003: 122)

Enquiry learning is a paradox. On the one hand we know how important it is, on the other it is difficult to encourage in an environment of targets and curriculum content which so often make it hard to achieve. The above quotation from De Botton could equally be about the primary geography curriculum. It comes from a chapter in which De Botton puzzles over why he, a philosopher, finds it so hard to be curious in a strange place, while others have shown persistent curiosity and wonder about their surroundings. While recognising that 'new facts' or 'incorrect facts' have traditionally driven enquiry, he ponders on how we can continue to enquire in a world where we are surrounded by 'facts'.

This chapter has been an attempt to identify opportunities in the geography National Curriculum to give children opportunities to participate in genuine enquiry, based on those areas of knowledge which still offer the potential to intrigue.

References

Bonnett, M. (1994) *Children's Thinking*. London: Cassell.

Bonnett, M. (2004) *Retrieving Nature: Education for a Post-Humanist Age*. Oxford: Blackwell.

Bridge, C. (2005) Around our school: The seagull's busy day. Geographical Association Superscheme Unit 1.

Catling, S. (2003) 'Curriculum contested. Primary geography and social justice', *Geography*, 88, July.

De Botton, A. (2003) *The Art of Travel*. Harmondsworth: Penguin.

Foley, M. (1999) 'Using enquiry: international research in geographical and environmental education', *Education*, 8 (1).

Higgins, S. and Baumfield, V. (2001) *Thinking Through Primary Teaching*. Cambridge: Chris Kington Publishing.

Leat, D. (2000) 'The importance of "big" concepts and skills, in learning geography', in Fisher, C. and Binns, T. (eds) *Issues in Geography Teaching*. London: Routledge.

Mackintosh, M. (2005) 'Talking about the last wilderness', *Primary Geographer*, Spring.

Riley, C. (1999) 'Evidence, understanding period knowledge and development of literacy, layers of inference at KS3', *Teaching History*, **97**, November.

Roberts, M. (1998) 'The nature of geographical enquiry at Key Stage 3', *Teaching Geography*, **23** (4), October.

Roberts, M. (2003) *Learning Through Enquiry*. Sheffield: Geographical Association.

Rowlands, S. (1984) *The enquiring classroom*. Lewes: Falmer Press.

Rowley, C. and Lewis, L. (2003) *Thinking on the Edge*. Kendal: Living Earth.

Sterling, S. (2001) *Sustainable Education, Revisioning Learning and Change*. Totnes: Green.

Storm, M. (1989) 'The five basic questions for primary geography', *Primary Geographer*, **2**, 4–5.

Taylor, L. (2004) *Re-presenting Geography*. Cambridge: Chris Kington Publishing.

Weblinks

Geographical Association 'Valuing Places' project,

www.geography.org.uk/valuingplaces

SAPERE (The Society to Advance Philosophical Enquiry and Reflection in Education)

www.sapere.org.uk

How can we plan effectively to foster progression in geographical understanding?

John Goodwin

> Geography teaching and learning should be an enjoyable, creative, stimulating and magical experience for pupils and teachers alike.
>
> (Richardson 2004: 303)

THE POTENTIAL OF the experiences that we group together under the heading of geography is illustrated by this quotation. The challenge for all teachers is to make that potential a reality for the children they teach. How does planning and preparing our geographical experiences in school help to develop that sense of magic, excitement, awe and wonder? On the face of it geography should be well suited to provide such experiences. Can anyone stand at the foot of a large waterfall and fail to be moved by the majesty and awesome power that is evident before their eyes? How can we fail but be impressed by big man-made structures such as suspension bridges and skyscrapers?

But geography has recently been identified as the weakest subject taught in the primary curriculum (QCA 2003/4). Despite the potential of the subject to excite, engage and inspire children, the evidence suggests that this is not happening in many primary schools. In response Lambert (2005) argues that geography 'concerns real world learning'. While we may wish to define 'real' more closely (for it may be that reality lies as much in stories as in images and text), it is clear that geography is grounded firmly in the experiences that we have, as we grow up. Geography lies at the heart of our relationship with the places and experiences that define our lives. As such, it should be at the centre of children's learning, not at the periphery. Can we make this happen?

A fresh look at the planning process

Do we teach enough geography? While geography might well appear on all school plans with sufficient regularity to ensure that the requirements of the National Curriculum are being met, is that really adequate for such an important subject? The reported weakness of geography, however, must often lie in the quality of the planning rather than the amount that is taught. This chapter looks at the relationship between the planning and the teaching, which are, of course, intimately related. It is at the planning stage that we must consider our approach to the teaching.

Recent advances in curriculum development mean that the planning cycle shown below will be familiar to all readers. It is not the intention of this chapter to rework this process. Instead we shall consider how the ways in which we engage with this cycle can be changed, so as to respond to the need for improvement in the quality of primary geography.

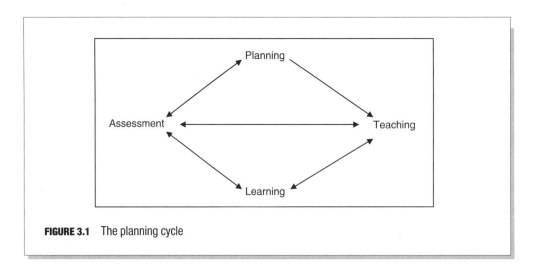

FIGURE 3.1 The planning cycle

The QCA schemes as a starting point for planning

The previous chapter looked at different ways of approaching the enquiry process which seek to change the way we think about geographical enquiry. Later chapters consider how geography relates to other areas of the curriculum. In this chapter we shall consider how planning can contribute to good learning experiences in geography, but also how the type of learning will influence the planning. Effective teaching is more than just delivering published strategies or schemes. It relies not just upon how they are linked to other aspects of the curriculum but, more importantly, on how creatively they are interpreted. We need to widen the concept of planning to embrace all the aspects involved in preparing to teach effectively. Organising and interpreting units of study from the QCA schemes (QCA 2000) are a key element of this process but it should also include consideration of the subject knowledge of the teachers, resources, links to other areas of study and creative opportunities available in the teaching.

Many or indeed most schools will be using the QCA programmes as the basis for their geography. Their use is beneficial in many ways. They identify how the requirements of the National Curriculum can be organised into easily accessed units of study, which can be planned across Key Stages, over a whole year. The schemes give definite guidance on what should be taught within each unit. Such prescription of what is to be taught will often be seen as a positive by teachers, particularly those who feel that they lack the knowledge to plan effectively for geography without support. Many would argue, however, that all teachers have an obligation to be creative. Creativity in the interpretation of QCA schemes should not be an optional extra, for it is only through creativity that inspirational teaching happens. The opportunity to be inventive with the geography schemes of work has to be grasped if we are to regain a strong position for geography in the primary curriculum. Geographical thinking is urgently needed as a context both for helping children to understand the world in which they grow up, and also in an increasingly interdependent global environment.

So how can we adapt and develop the sort of questions highlighted in the QCA schemes? The following two examples show how existing schemes offer opportunities for developing depth by adapting to local circumstances, firstly in the 'Village in India' scheme (Unit 10) and, secondly the 'Investigating Rivers' scheme (Unit 14) (QCA 2000).

A village in India

If a scheme such as Unit 10 is to be used successfully in a way which enables us to monitor children's progression, we must first identify the specific skills and concepts that we wish to focus upon. Here is a scheme with huge possibilities and numerous resources. So much is available that there is a real danger of trying to do too much.

It is common for 'similarity and difference' to be the key concept where both KS1 and KS2 look at a village in India. How would this concept be considered progressively with different key stages, ages and abilities? At one level assessing similarity and difference can be simply 'list making' (identifying different types of building materials used in Chembakolli and in the children's home area, for example). One form of conceptual progression comes when we relate these similarities and differences to the environment (where do the materials come from?), the economy (are the materials made locally or are they transported in?) and to the society (what influence do the materials have on the nature of the village and how people live their lives?).

Recognising conceptual progression enables us to design a scheme appropriate to children's age and ability. An excellent example of this can be seen in the way that the Geographical Association's 'super scheme' for this unit has identified a range of activities which each offer very different assessment opportunities based upon clear concepts: knowing how change might occur; observing how places are linked; recognising similarities and differences between rural locations in India (much more fairly comparable than the usual comparison with our home place); offering a critique of a brochure. Although each of these enables very different talents to be demonstrated, there is no particular linear progression, which is typical of much geographical work where our starting point is more likely to be the most motivating rather than the simplest, conceptually.

Investigating rivers

In the same way that the study of an Indian village should be planned around what motivates rather than what appears to be conceptually simple, so the study of a river should be determined by interest and motivation first.

Notwithstanding changes in guidelines for educational visits, there is still a major benefit in visiting a river. Where a visit is not possible, however, there are ways in which the study of a river can be enriched by, for example, developing a small river system in the school grounds. Though not always possible, it is surprising how easy this can be done with a small mound of bare earth or sand. The main channel should follow the natural flow (which can be found by pouring water at the top of the slope) and observing its flow. This pattern can then be used to carve a small channel and thus create the main river channel. Since this is a natural process it should replicate the processes involved in an actual river and repeated use of it will show areas of erosion and deposition and illustrate such features as meanders. It can be developed further to include other streams to link in and show features such as tributaries and confluences. Increasing the flow will simulate the processes involved when rivers flood, with the channel running faster and with more force and flooding its banks, creating an area which is in effect its flood plain. Under certain circumstances it will be possible to simulate the time lag between high rainfall in one area and the flood effects lower downstream. If such a project is not possible in the grounds, similar but smaller models can be created in the classroom using a sand tray, providing there is a drain hole in one end with a bucket to collect water leaving the tray.

Going beyond the QCA schemes

In using the QCA schemes as a basis for development there are two factors we need first to consider: the existing relationship between geography and other subjects, and the Excellence and Enjoyment strategy (DfES 2003).

Relationship of geography to other subjects

One of the constraints placed on curriculum development has been the requirement within the National Literacy Strategy (DfEE 1998) and the National Numeracy

Strategy (DfEE 1999) for dedicated daily periods of language and mathematics work. The National Curriculum is presented in terms of separate subjects and so it is understandable that in many schools this has prompted the development of a fragmented timetable similar to that used in secondary schools. This may well result in foundation subjects being covered only once a week and some subjects may not be taught at all in some terms. This structure may well ensure that all subjects are represented in the curriculum and that some kind of curriculum balance is achieved.

But is this necessarily the best way for children to learn? Is there pedagogical evidence to support such a fragmented approach for such young children? Is it a structure that has emerged from the need to be seen to cover every subject? There is an increasing awareness now of the conceptual basis behind geography as a subject. Concepts such as interdependence, diversity, change, location and pattern, among others, offer the opportunity to reintegrate geography with other subjects, while at the same time maintaining a rigour that enables us to develop progressive planning (see below). Attempts at producing combined units by the QCA (such as combining geography and history or geography and science, both of which are offered on the QCA website) fail to identify the distinctiveness of each subject and are in danger of returning to a lack of conceptual rigour which was said (though not necessarily the case in much good practice at that time) to characterise pre-National Curriculum topic-led work.

A successful combined scheme needs to demonstrate how each subject will build on the conceptual rigour of the other subject. In addition, success in combining schemes will come from looking for opportunities to develop children's thinking, collaboration and critical skills. It is easy to allow these terms to become tokenistic and there are many approaches to developing such skills. Fundamentally however, most teachers would like to see a progression in children's ability to think about their own learning, to develop a clear meta-cognitive approach to their learning alongside an openness to learn from and alongside others.

Grasmere School in Cumbria, for example, combine history and geography on a visit to the coast with a clear sense of developing those reflective skills through dialogue and philosophy for children. On a visit to the beach they encountered Victorian rubbish which was revealed in a salt marsh as a result of changing currents in Morecambe Bay. While, in this case, the geographical processes in the Bay provided a sound conceptual basis for developing knowledge and understanding, the difference in attitudes to rubbish between the Victorians and our own generation provided an excellent stimulus for a whole-class philosophical enquiry into the nature of rubbish, and also linked to work on Victorian Britain. The key has to be planning which has the fundamentals there, but which looks for fresh opportunities each year to offer a stimulus for real learning. Another year it was the route of the footpath through the school grounds, once a necessity but increasingly a liability, a brilliant opportunity for a combined history and geography enquiry into a dilemma where the solution is not certain.

Excellence and Enjoyment

Each school will respond to the Excellence and Enjoyment initiative (DfES 2003) in a different way, but a common thread will be to make use of the freedom to consider how the curriculum can be organised in a more flexible way. The Literacy and Numeracy Strategies on the one hand, and the Excellence and Enjoyment strategy on the other, have important implications for the further development of QCA schemes. Below are several approaches to planning which take them into account. In particular we need to consider the implications of blocked time, continuous units and opportunities for outdoor work in ensuring that geography planning encourages excellence and enjoyment.

Planning for blocked time

The freedom offered by the Excellence and Enjoyment strategy means that schools are now in a position to feel more confident about organising large blocks of time. This is not to argue that everything should be taught in super topics but that it is a position to be considered. However this should be more than just lumping together two or three history, geography and design and technology units linked by a topic title, then teaching them as a separate subject within the theme. We need to consider how studying this topic will develop the geographical thinking of the children we teach. How will I need to arrange the learning experiences to enable genuine and natural connections to be made between subjects?

The QCA units give guidance on the number of hours for each. These do not need to be spread evenly over a term. There is scope to block different experiences together so that a geographical project may be carried out over three or four afternoons (assuming mathematics and English take place every morning) and that in subsequent weeks similar emphasis is given to other subjects. At the end of the term each area of study would have been covered.

It is inevitable that events occur which cannot be foreseen and that all planned sessions will not be taught. Anecdotal evidence would suggest that it is the foundation subjects (including geography) that are more likely to be dropped rather than one of the core subjects. But that would represent 100 per cent of a foundation subject planned for that week. Yet this would be only 20 per cent of time planed for mathematics or English that week. The grouping of geography sessions together over a shorter period would alleviate the impact of such occurrences.

Such an approach has other advantages. It allows for a concentration of energy and enthusiasm by both children and staff and a shared objective. In practical work a finished product is achieved more quickly without the problem of storing half finished artefacts. It allows for easier provision for children with special educational needs at either end of the ability spectrum. Those children identified as being more able can more easily develop the skills of independence and reflection over a longer period of study than they can within a fragmented approach.

Children cannot always retain piecemeal knowledge from one week to the next. So much time can be wasted reminding them of what was covered previously. Working on the same theme on successive days allows children to consolidate and develop their understanding. On a practical note, it makes sense to have models, artefacts or artworks that require a substantial amount of time to create to be 'in progress' for only a week rather than for five weeks but only worked on once a week. It can also help children focus more closely on the concepts involved and allow those children who need more time to consolidate to do so in an unpressured way.

The following example looks at how geography could be linked to design and technology, in a topic combining bridges and rivers in a blocked and combined theme. The topic of bridges may be an appropriate area of study involving consideration of structures, materials, fixatives, etc., and can fulfil key learning objectives of the design and technology curriculum. However, there is also scope to consider what bridges are used for and, more importantly, where (over roads, railways, canals and rivers).

This latter consideration provides a pertinent link to a consideration of how the behaviour of a river can influence the nature of a bridge built to cross it. Rivers are not static, as are roads or railways, and so *how* they change needs to be taken into account when designing and building bridges. River flow varies greatly, especially when in flood, so how do we design a bridge that can account for such changes? To answer this, children will need to either apply what they have already learned to inform their thoughts or use this as a starting point to find out *how* the river may change. (In certain areas of Southern Europe bridges have to be built to span a wide flood plain although for most of the year they appear to be superfluous to the visible channel.)

If this work is based around a local bridge then such a study will contribute to study of the local area. This would then open up opportunities for the introduction of an historical consideration to the study. Why was a bridge built here in the first place? Why were those materials used? If we built another bridge today would it look the same? Why, or why not? (There is evidence to suggest the Romans were able to ford the Humber but it was not until the twentieth century that the technology allowed a bridge to be built.)

Planning for continuous units

Some of the units within the QCA scheme are written as continuous. Planning for the inclusion of these units raises special issues which may explain why they are not commonly taught. Appropriate coverage of these units inevitably requires some degree of flexibility. Snow of any appreciable amount is rare in many parts of the country but when it does snow there is a brilliant opportunity to extend children's experiences in many ways. It cannot be seen as good teaching to ignore it completely because snow does not occur at that time in our planning. If geography (or indeed any area of study) is about the real world we need to be ready to seize these opportunities. If we take them seriously they are a key element of the overall provision. We can perhaps accept that this would be one of the roles of the geography co-ordinator, who needs to find ways of ensuring that colleagues know how to include such events when they occur, and that this is allowed and indeed, desirable. How then does the co-ordinator ensure that such events are able to be included in the curriculum?

One continuous unit (Unit 16 What's in the News? (QCA 2000)) raises particular issues. What sort of events are likely to occur in the news? Unfortunately those that readily spring to mind tend to be those of a catastrophic nature, such as a tsunami, hurricanes or flooding. Given that the treatment of this tends to be of the negative view, how do we plan to treat these issues in the primary classroom? Flooding is most certainly a horrific and anguishing experience but can the impact of such an occurrence be avoided? Is there not scope to help children see that building in flood plains is not a good idea! At the time of writing, a series of mud slides in Guatamala (a result of hurricane Katrina) have claimed the lives of thousands of people. This occurred both as a direct result of the mud slides and an inability to bring relief to the survivors owing to the roads having been obliterated. It is an easy response to discuss this in an assembly and perhaps make a collection to aid the relief effort, but should we not be extending the children's understanding of why a relief effort is needed in the first place? Some awareness of the geography of the region, alongside other considerations, is vital to a full understanding of the situation. Without it there is a danger that the serious consequences of such phenomena are seen to be what happens to people who live abroad. Continuous units are often harder to build in to planning, but it may be that they cover some of the most important aspects of the geography curriculum.

Planning for outdoor work

One of the key areas that may be said to distinguish geography from other subjects is that it requires some work outdoors, in the field. If we deny this then we are in danger of reducing the study to an academic exercise and thus restricting our scope for magic and excitement. Notwithstanding recent changes in legislation, purposeful outdoor experiences can be planned and implemented, as shown in Chapter 4. Many schools plan for outdoor experiences, with emphasis on adventure activities. There is much scope to plan for developing geographical understanding within such activities without having a geography lesson.

Recent safety legislation may appear to put a brake on such direct experiences for some teachers, so the challenge is to plan within existing guidelines to ensure that children are not deprived of such opportunities. Recently, for example, I joined a class of primary school children on a ghyll scrambling expedition. All the risks had been assessed. For the children the focus of the morning was the adventure of scrambling up a ghyll (a mountain stream for those who do not live in Cumbria!). But they were also gaining a direct understanding of what it feels like to be physically in a river, in the early stages of its existence. They discussed how it sounded. They could feel, as well as see, how the water had eroded the rocks. They took photographs to record what the place was like.

Back in school they had an incentive to find the place on a map. This involved finding the co-ordinate reference. They could relate the ghyll on the map to their experience. Now that they understood how to read contours and co-ordinates, could they identify any similar areas which would be suitable for ghyll scrambling? The more able pupils were given the task of identifying transport links in order to decide if it would be possible to get to any of the newly identified sites. This led to a discussion about conservation issues; were there any reasons for limiting ghyll scrambling adventures? The discriminating reader will have seen that there were many opportunities for music, English and art as well!

Planning for enquiry in geography

The grid shown in Figure 3.2 is suggested as an approach to planning a sequence of enquiry lessons which will incorporate the elements of enquiry skills that have been identified in Chapter 2. It is based on the notion that in order to understand the world we need to use different 'ways of knowing', not purely logical ones. While basing each lesson on a concept and a skill, it also asks that we plan over time in such a way that more intuitive and less rational learning (particularly in considering a sense of wonder and aesthetics) takes place, alongside more rational and logical learning (for example, in considering issues of ethics and fairness but also more normally in the more scientific aspects of geography – as in exploring how the natural environment works).

There are a variety of ways of using this approach, either for planning a specific scheme to ensure that a variety of approaches are used or by linking types of enquiry to different types of trigger or stimulus for the enquiry.

Example of a medium-term plan using this approach to enquiry

The theme of the enquiry was, 'A trip to the coast'. The focus was on developing a sense of what makes this place special.

The three lessons that follow are intended to develop wonder (lesson 1, Figure 3.3), an appreciation of beauty (lesson 2, Figure 3.4), ethics and fairness (lesson 3, Figure 3.5) and logic (lesson 4, Figure 3.6).

These lessons have implications for how enquiry is planned in the curriculum. To be successful they need a planning and assessment framework which recognises 'different ways of knowing' and which looks at progression of conceptual

	Ways of Knowing			
	Intuitive inner person enquiry Individual values			Logical and deductive outer person enquiry Group values
	Wonder	*Aesthetics*	*Ethics*	*Logic*
What is this place like?				
Concept				
Skill				
Knowledge				
Why is it like that?				
Concept				
Skill				
Knowledge				
How is this place connected to other places?				
Concept				
Skill				
Knowledge				
How is this place changing?				
Concept				
Skill				
Knowledge				
What would it feel like to live in this place?				
Concept				
Skill				
Knowledge				

FIGURE 3.2 Planning grid using different ways of knowing to develop geographical enquiry skills

Year 4
Key concept: Special places
Skill: Identifying similarities and differences
Trigger for enquiry: A visit to a place which is in some way special; in this case a beach
National Curriculum link: Describe and explain how and why places are similar to and different to other places

Actvity: A story, poem or statement is read that in some way relates to the special nature of the place.

Exercise: A list of places (the seaside, your bedroom, a wild place, a busy place, a den, etc.) and a list of words which might describe why a place is special (friends, quiet, lonely, comfortable, noisy, exciting, etc.). Children choose a place and some words from the list plus any others that they want. Place them on a map that they draw of the place. All the classes' responses can then be compared and contrasted to see how we use both similar and different types of reasons for our choices of special place.

The concept of special places
Geography is consistently asking why some places seem to be preferred to others. If we could answer that many other puzzles about the relationship between human behaviour and the environment would fit into place. Why do we travel to particular places? Why do we place particular meaning on some places and not others? These and other questions form the bedrock of understanding pattern and process in the subject.

The skill of identifying similarities and differences
Being able to observe what makes places similar and different is not a simple case of looking. We need to learn how to look. Often it is a case of seeing what isn't there as much as what is. Comparing the places chosen as special in this exercise offers an opportunity to see how we use both similar and different reasons for our choice.

FIGURE 3.3 Focus on a sense of wonder (developed from the planning grid in Figure 3.2)

Year 4
Key concept: Beauty
Skill: Reasoning with values
Trigger for enquiry: Pictures taken during a visit to the beach
National Curriculum link: Identify and describe what places are like

Activity: Using the images, various activities are possible:
1. Each child is asked to find one thing that is ugly in the picture. They then pass it to a neighbour who has to find something that is beautiful in the same picture. This is continued with all the images. Then, in discussion, questions are raised about how we decide whether a place is beautiful or ugly. One question is chosen for class discussion.
2. Each group is asked to take on the role of manager of a photographic gallery. They are given three walls and must decide which images, and how many, will go on each wall, and say how they decided. What other ways are there of grouping these? What skills did each group use to decide? How do we decide on reasons and are some reasons better than others?

The concept of beauty
Beauty is an example of one of those concepts which is almost entirely value led, and yet at the same time we have many common criteria for beauty. It is an ideal concept for an enquiry because there are so many ways of deciding and all depend on good reasoning of different types.

The skill of reasoning with values
Even value-laden words demand us to give reasons why we think that way. Giving a reason why we see a landscape or place as having beauty might involve a range of emotions, from excitement and danger to colour and texture. If we are to challenge and consider our interaction with the environment we must first learn why we show preferences. When is a town more beautiful than the countryside? Imagine how our urban sprawl and transport requirements would change if more of us were able to appreciate beauty in different ways, free from our assumptions.

FIGURE 3.4 Focus on aesthetics and beauty (developed from planning grid in Figure 3.2)

Year 4
Key concept: Interdependence
Skill: Evaluating
Trigger for enquiry: Possible influences on an issue that is happening at the coast, e.g. cockles are disappearing, the cliff is wearing away, the dunes are being destroyed
National Curriculum link: Recognise how places fit within a wider geographical context and are interdependent

Activity: Provide a list of possible causes of the change, some created locally and others caused by something out of our control or far away. In groups, decide and give reasons for which factors you think have caused the change.

Exercise:

	Changes in our control	Changes out of our control
The beach		
The tide		
The cliffs		
The water		
The number of cockles		

The concept of interdependence
If the study of other places is to have any reason beyond curiosity it is likely that interdependence would be the key concept. Any decision that we now make in terms of how we shop, travel and work is likely to have a global impact. To begin to understand how places rely on each other as well as effect each other is central to appreciating our relationship to the environment.

The skill of evaluating
Most geographical relationships require us to decide which factors are most influential. In this example an ethical factor is introduced. Are some changes in our control. If so, who is responsible for those changes?

FIGURE 3.5   Focus on ethics (developed from planning grid in Figure 3.2)

Year 4
Key concept: Cause and effect
Skill: Reasoning
Trigger for enquiry: The issue already identified, e.g. how might one factor, in this case the tide, have effected the place?
National Curriculum link: Recognise physical and human processes and explain how these can cause change

Activity: Focus on the tide and how it changes over time (see bbc.co.uk/marine for local tidal changes). Explore the pattern of the tides (no need to explain why it is like that) and try to match those to the patterns on the beach. What else might be influencing these patterns (wind, etc.).

Exercise: Children asked to decide on particular shapes they could make on the ground if they wanted to explain to some extraterrestrials in space how the tide changes, e.g.

The concept of cause and effect
Geography has a strong scientific link and part of that is the subject's interest in the physical as well as the human reasons for patterns. Some of that can be explained by straightforward cause and effect reasoning. The beach has many patterns on it, either in stones or in the sand. These patterns are replaced daily and many are a result of the tide, whatever state it happens to be in at the time.

The skill of reasoning logically
At KS2 we may not want to explain the tide, a complex planetary interaction. Before understanding tides, however, we do need to observe the pattern through time (daily and monthly patterns of occurrence). There are many ways of interpreting these patterns, some more logical than others. The exercise here is an opportunity to make different representations of the patterns that a simple tidal graph from the internet reveals.

FIGURE 3.6   Focus on logic (developed from planning grid in Figure 3.2)

understanding alongside skill development. Figure 3.2 is one possible approach to such planning, while maintaining a link to the key questions approach used by QCA schemes.

Assessment and progression

In researching this chapter a common theme was the difficulty with the issue of assessing geography. Do we assess geographical awareness in all its forms or do we identify specific aspects such as knowledge, conceptual awareness and ethical development?

Assessment seems a very simple concept: What did I want the children to learn? Did they learn it? We can complicate this with consideration of success criteria, recording mechanisms and so on, but these are of no use if we cannot find useful ways of assessing how children have benefited from a learning experience.

Why should there be a problem with assessing children's geographical development but not so with their mathematical development? Is there anything intrinsic to geography that makes assessment any more difficult than in mathematics?

The answer would appear to lie in the way that geography teaching is approached. If it is just delivering the published schemes without considering the underlying geographical pedagogy then there is likely to be a major problem in assessment. If we do not know what we want them to learn, then it is difficult to decide whether they have achieved it.

This then brings us back to the issue of subject knowledge. The problem with geography is that subject knowledge is so often seen in purely factual knowledge terms. The examples illustrated above, together with those in the previous chapter, indicate that it is conceptual knowledge that is most important in understanding assessment and progression in geographical understanding.

Chapter 2 identified a number of key concepts in geography and suggested a way of planning to include these in enquiries. A school which identifies these concepts as central to the breadth of geography can plan for a progression through ensuring that the key concepts and skills are embedded in the curriculum to enable a progressive growth of children's ability to engage with geography at increasingly sophisticated levels.

Conclusion

Planning progression and assessment cannot be separated from the approach to teaching and learning. The approach to learning has huge implications for the organisation of the learning experiences for children within the geography curriculum. Recent changes in curriculum requirements should allow for such a revision of our provision. Such modifications should concentrate on a shared clear view of the geographical understanding that we wish to develop within the children and a flexibility in approach closely matched to the needs and experiences of the children.

This chapter has recognised that planning, progression and assessment cannot be separated from 'how we teach' as well as 'what we teach'. How we interpret QCA schemes, how we ensure excellence and enjoyment through planning for blocked schemes, continuous units, outdoor work and enquiry is influenced by our view of what geography is and how it should be taught.

References

DfEE (1998) *The National Literacy Strategy*. London: DfEE.

DfEE (1999) *The National Numeracy Strategy*. London: DfEE.

DfES (2003) *Excellence and Enjoyment: A Strategy for Primary Schools*. London: DfES.

Geographical Association (2006) *Super Schemes* (available from www.geography.org.uk).

Lambert, D. (2005) 'An axis to grind', Opinion, *Times Educational Supplement*, 4 March.

QCA (2000) A Scheme of Work for Key Stages 1 and 2: Geography (The Standards Site www.standards.dfes.gov.uk/schemes2).

QCA (2003/4) Ofsted Primary Subject Report (www.qca.org.uk).

Richardson, P. (2004) 'Planning the geography curriculum', in Scoffham, S. (ed.) *Primary Geography Handbook*. Sheffield: Geographical Association, p. 303.

Concepts of place

Sustainable education: what's that all about and what has geography fieldwork got to do with it?

Chris Buxton

A 'SUSTAINABLE EDUCATION' will be one which balances 'heart, head and hand', and integrates 'person, people and place'. In this chapter I explain what I mean by this definition and then discuss the implications for fieldwork in geography.

Where are we now?

Our current 'modern' Way of Being – that is, how we emotionally 'feel', intellectually 'think' and practically 'act', in relation to ourselves, each other and our environment – is leading us inexorably to an unsustainable way of living in an unsustainable world, and is arguably the major cause of the wide variety of psychological, social and environmental crises which we now face, both as individuals and as a global community.

There are fundamental reasons why this is so. The first reason that I put forward is presented in Figure 4.1.

We have lost the balance between the inner and outer aspects of our lives, which are necessary to be fully human and truly sustainable. We have allowed the thinking, rational, 'knowledgeable', intellectual outer dimensions of our lives (expressed largely through the 'sciences') to dominate while much of the feeling, intuitive, 'passionate', emotional, inner dimensions of our lives (expressed largely through the 'arts') are dismissed as being of little relevance, or have come to be ignored or distrusted. The result is that we have reached a situation where we

> Our current Way of Being has created an imbalance between
>
> **the way we feel (Heart)** and **the way we think (Head)**
>
> the 'affective' (aesthetic and ethical) and the 'scientific' dimensions of our lives
>
> with implications for
>
> **the way we act (Hand)**
>
> the 'practical' dimension

FIGURE 4.1   Our current Way of Being

intellectually know more than ever about our crises, and their potential consequences, but we do not emotionally care about them, or, if we do care, we are left overwhelmed and helpless in our desire to act.

We depend on intellectual knowledge to inform our actions, but need emotional commitment to drive them. No matter how much we are rationally aware of an issue, we are only likely to act and protect that which we intuitively love.

And so we continue to talk about sustainability, while living unsustainably. We amass more and more knowledge about our world, but without the passion, wisdom or responsibility 'to see that it is well used in the world' (Orr 1994: 13). We are able to rationally discuss the dangers of sea level rise or the relationship between air pollution and the incidence of childhood asthma without any real commitment to acting on it. We continue to develop the outer 'scientific' aspects of our lives at the expense of the inner 'affective' (aesthetic and ethical) aspects, with the result that we are not fully 'whole' people.

We are denying ourselves a fundamental part of what it means to be human and yet, as Sterling (2001) argues, it is only by becoming more human, that we can become more sustainable. Can we afford then, to be 'emotionless' in our dealings with our intellect any longer?

Secondly, one fundamental outcome of this overemphasis on the rational over the intuitive aspects of our lives is the separation that now exists between ourselves/each other; the earth; environment, nature; and our spirituality, as depicted in Figure 4.2.

As an animal species we have an innate connection to our 'natural' world as part of our evolutionary heritage and are totally embedded in and dependent upon it as our one and only life support system. This connection could be seen as a critical component of our sense of place, sense of belonging, and sense of identity, however unknowingly, and as such is fundamental to our well-being.

However, humankind has become progressively separated from that 'natural' world and from much of what makes us human such that now, as John Muir

---

Ourselves Each Other
(Person) (People)
and our

Earth/Environment/Nature
(Place)
and

Our Spirituality
(Spirit)

and much of how we now act is a result of that perceived separation

FIGURE 4.2   Perceived separation

(John Muir Award 2001) noted, 'most people are on the world, not in it – have no conscious sympathy or relationship to anything about them – undiffused, separate, and rigidly alone like marbles of polished stone'.

This deep psychological and physical separation, compounded by our rational attempts to make sense of our world, has led to the fragmentation of life into small, specialised, distinct, isolated, 'boxed' compartments, or the 'Many', divorced from our intuitive way of seeing the world as a 'seamless whole', or the 'One'.

Making distinctions has been a helpful stage in developing understanding but it is almost as if we have forgotten that the way we divide the world up into abstract concepts is for our own convenience, and not the way the world really is. As a consequence, we have come to see such concepts as being real in themselves. It would seem that such an approach has now outlived its usefulness as it has become increasingly far removed from our actual experience of the world as being integrative, transdisciplinary and interdependent – one unity made up of diversity – both One and Many.

Much of our way of life, education and language continues to reinforce these abstract divisions in which inherently connected aspects have come to be seen as totally separate entities, in spite of the growing awareness of the adverse effects of such a view. So it is, for example, that formal schooling has a multitude of highly specialised and rigidly divided disciplines, exemplified by the National Curriculum in particular, which encourages fragmented thinking and knowledge and results in students graduating 'without any broad integrated sense of the unity of things' (Orr 1994: 11).

Foremost among these abstract divisions is the fundamental one we make between ourselves as humans and the earth we inhabit, illustrated through terms such as:

Humankind	and 'The environment'
People	and Planet
Human geography	and Physical Geography
'Indoors'	and 'Outdoors'
Classroom work	and Fieldwork

as if they somehow existed separately from each other.

The idea of 'saving the earth' is indicative of this divide in that it maintains the illusion of separation between humankind and the environment rather than addressing the crucial issue of humankind's behaviour as an integral part of that earth. It is not the earth that needs to be saved; it is humankind from itself.

Our perceived separation might not be so crucial but for the fact that it allows us to act in ways which in any other context would be deemed insane. Destroying our own oxygen production system, polluting our own water supplies, eliminating our own sources of food and denying ourselves any meaning to life are not life-enhancing actions, and yet we are hard at work doing exactly that and, perhaps of greater concern, educating our children to do the same, only better.

This state of disconnection, as Richard Louv (2005) points out, is likely to worsen as we now face the prospect of our first 'nature deficit disorder' generation; a generation who will have little if any meaningful contact with the natural world that supports them.

Perhaps most fundamentally of all, we are experiencing a separation from our own spirituality; that which gives us life, makes us truly alive and gives meaning to all we do.

Our current 'modern' Way of Being has culminated in the intellectual dominance of 'being' and the human dominance of nature, which are now no longer proving adequate means to make sense of our experience of the world and our place in it. It has allowed us to act in ways that go counter to our deep intuitive and innate natural sense; to act 'inhumanly' and 'unnaturally'.

Is it any wonder then that we have a society in which so many people are living lost, empty, alienated, lonely, soulless, disconnected, meaningless lives, and where truancy, depression, bullying, aggression and stress are some of the prevalent symptoms in our modern world . . . and classrooms . . .? Can we go on in a transdisciplinary world without a transdisciplinary outlook? Are forms of separation and disintegration all we have got to look forward to?

Our current education system, in spite of its presumed role as a 'lever for change', arguably sustains and promotes our unsustainable Way of Being, with the result that we are in danger of creating 'well-educated' citizens who are just more effective and 'successful' at exploiting others and the earth, rather than encouraging the development of well-educated citizens who can live more sustainable lifestyles. It is a system that generates a surfeit of experience and knowledge contributing to unsustainability, and insufficient experience and knowledge about how to live sustainably. Is that what we, as educators, really want it to be? Can we afford, for the sake of all human and non-human kind, for it to be like that?

Our current geography discipline, as an integral part of this education system, could currently be viewed as just a marginal and largely ineffective by-product of such a system which, in spite of some valiant efforts to the contrary, makes little contribution overall to challenging a Way of Being that is ultimately threatening to us all.

Some of the children you are now teaching are likely to be around beyond the year 2100. Will they be facing a world in darkness and under water? How will they feel about the world they are inheriting ... and how would we justify our actions to them? As 'Geographers', members of the great integrative discipline, surely it is incumbent on us to do something about it. If we don't, who will?

Where do we want to be?

What then might be a new 'sustainable' Way of Being? Firstly, any new 'sustainable' Way of Being must seek to balance the feeling (heart) and thinking (head) aspects in respect of any action (hand) we take, allowing us to realise our full potential as individuals and as global citizens. When we are able to feel from the 'heart', as well as we know from the 'head', then there is hope for positive change.

Secondly, we need to raise our ways of feeling, thinking and acting to a higher level that allows us to reconnect with, rather than separate from, the wider human and non-human world of which we are already an integral part.

Ultimately the divisive man-made boundaries between these will then gradually merge and become integrated as we open up to a Way of Being that is by its very nature sustainable. It will not be a case of choosing whether or not to live sustainably, we will just *be* sustainable.

Such a Way of Being would mean that many of the questions and challenges we now face would just not arise, our current divisive way of living would be seen for the insanity and nonsense that it is, and the only possible and inevitable course of action would be that which contributed to the integrity of people and planet.

It will require a courageous leap into the 'void' that will challenge the very sense of who we are, and who we want to be, both individually and collectively. Do we jump before we are pushed? . . . And what role has education got to play in this?

So, any form of 'sustainable education' will need to

(a) Create opportunities to involve children in ways of learning that are predominantly intuitive or non-rational (developing 'emotional literacy'), along with appropriate rational aspects of knowledge and understanding (developing 'ecological literacy'), both of which are necessary to inform our actions.

(b) Seek the ways and means to integrate these and set them within the context of our earthly and spiritual worlds, as the basis for transformative experiences that can lead towards sustainability.

In so doing, it will need a much greater emphasis on, and trust in, the *process* of education, rather than on the content, as is currently the case; on the ways we teach and learn, rather than what we teach and learn.

What role has geography got to play in this?

'I feel that geography is the most basic subject in the curriculum. Without geography you are nowhere! It embraces all of the subjects in the National Curriculum . . . If children do not learn about where we are and how we survive from the earth's resources, then they will be inadequate to make their own choices in how we live and treat the environment . . . Above all, geography should develop their sense of awe and wonder of the world around them and their responsibility to look after it.'

(Trainee teacher – Cumbria)

Geography's strength lies in its ability to unite the world of human activity with the natural earth and as such it is uniquely placed to be a contributory factor to a 'sustainable' Way of Being. It has the integrative potential to:

(a) Balance those aspects of respect and love for the world we live in with knowledge of the social and natural processes that operate within it. This is primarily through its role as a bridge between the humanities and sciences and with its capacity for trans-disciplinary study.

(b) Connect humans with their world through the opportunities it offers for practical engagement with 'person, people and place', at a variety of scales from local to global.

'Geography is a fantastic educational resource with extraordinary potential for informing future citizens' (Lambert 2005), and is 'the one subject whose main focus is on identifying the big picture, drawing together the strands which explain where, why and how, and examining relationships between the natural and human worlds' (Rawling 2005).

The potential is there, and it would be an opportunity for geography to re-establish its value by responding honestly, coherently and responsibly in providing the overarching perspective sustainability demands. It will however, need to go well beyond its current state if it is to create the truly life-changing experiences that will be necessary if we are to meet our present and future needs.

Could it be that geography could come to see itself not so much as one of many 'subjects' fighting for space in an overcrowded school timetable but as the vanguard, or the forerunner, of the 'sustainable' Way of Being we so desperately need? In effect, as an integrating form of education which offered a genuinely balanced and broad curriculum, and equally engaged our affective and scientific dimensions in the context of a wider all encompassing world. It would mean geography taking a stand and fully utilising its strength in providing the vision, sense of direction and articulation of both the map and route necessary. It would mean geography actually putting the integrity of us as people and of the planet ahead of defending the integrity of subject disciplines, but ultimately what is vastly more important? So what on earth has geography fieldwork got to do with all that?

How are we going to get there?

How might geography fieldwork contribute to a 'sustainable' Way of Being?

If geography is to be in the forefront of generating positive action for change towards a 'sustainable' Way of Being, and we see fieldwork as being a fundamental part of that, then we need to review the form that such fieldwork will take – more of the same is no longer an option.

So, what are the most effective ways of developing both children's emotional and intellectual capacities, that is, what experiences will encourage children to engage in their world with an open heart as well as an open mind, such that they are then motivated to act positively on the combination of passion and knowledge resulting from that? And, how do we help children realise that they are an integral part of the planet on which they are totally dependent? In essence, geography just needs to get back to doing what it does best, but within a new framework for new times – enquiry in relation to a place. It is hard to believe it sounds that simple, but let us see that as a positive and encouraging sign.

Enquiry: enquiry within and enquiry without

Enquiry is a natural aspect of a child's development and fundamental to our understanding of the world, but to be effective and relevant it must now encompass both enquiry within and enquiry without (see Figure 4.3), and, equally importantly, the means to draw these together as a whole.

Much of current primary geography fieldwork tends to focus on the 'scientific' 'observe and record' type of process, which is valuable and essential within its own terms, but is only one part of a much bigger picture. It is now no longer sufficient to go and undertake geographical studies from the 'outside in'; we need to equally undertake them from the 'inside out', and then bring those perspectives together.

Enquiry 'within'	Enquiry 'without'
(aesthetic/ethical forms of enquiry)	(scientific forms of enquiry)

FIGURE 4.3 Enquiry types

If fieldwork enquiry is to help us create the comprehensive overview our global society so desperately needs, then it must begin to draw on and integrate all our faculties as both people and geographers.

> 'I believe that the essential part of children learning geography in primary school is investigation. The curriculum should allow children to engage in experiential learning and the chance to make sense of geography for themselves at some stages, as well as being guided by the teachers in others.'
>
> (Trainee teacher – Cumbria)

Any such 'investigation' must be one that encourages going into the 'depths of things', however; to generate the right questions before we can begin to think about the right answers.

Place: get outdoors and explore!

Experiential learning connecting to place

When was the last time you walked barefoot, got 'lost' in yourself, saw beauty in the ordinary, experienced being 'wild', travelled like a bumble bee or thought like a mountain? How much do we really know of our own places? How can you know about the 'life' of a river or village if you have never experienced one? How often do we go and 'study' a place instead of immersing ourselves in it? Personal engagement with, and direct first-hand experience of, a real place is crucial to developing the higher levels of feeling and thinking necessary for 'opening new worlds and new ways of seeing that world' (Osbourne 2005), and of developing the motivation necessary to act on behalf of both our own and our planet's well-being.

Children need the opportunity to really connect to and love a place, somewhere they can experience and develop an affinity for, be part of and within, rather than apart from and without. That bond with a deep and natural part of our being can provide the motivation to want to act to care for the local place and the wider world beyond (deep emotional 'literacy'), as well as to develop the understanding of how it works and our role in it (deep ecological 'literacy'). Without an emotional affection for our own place, why should we be interested in caring for anyone else's? Without an ecological understanding of the interdependent nature of our place, why should we even consider 'joined up' thinking?

Ultimately, as a society can we afford not to undertake such fieldwork?

What are potential frameworks for fieldwork?

What frameworks for fieldwork are there that might offer a starting point towards a new 'sustainable' Way of Being; that is, frameworks that allow opportunity for the development of aspects of both 'enquiry within and without', and 'experiential learning connecting to place'?

Summarised below are just four alternative examples that might be usefully applied or adapted within the context of geography in a role as the vanguard of change. The source material is derived from the organisations themselves and through their websites.

The John Muir Award Scheme

The John Muir Award (JMA) is a national environmental award scheme that originated in Scotland, and is now being extended throughout England and Wales to encourage people of all ages to discover, enjoy, value, conserve and take responsibility for wild places in a spirit of fun, adventure and exploration. It is non-competitive and open to all and is being used by schools at both Key Stages 1 and 2. Gaining an Award involves meeting four challenges.

Discovering a wild place on which to focus your activity – The wild place (or places) can be anywhere, close to home or further afield: a local pond, park, beach, school grounds, nature reserve, a wildlife garden, a National Park or wilderness area. The aim is to experience it directly, enjoy it, and become familiar with it.

Exploring its natural and wild characteristics – Finding out what makes it special by 'tuning' into it and exploring it. This can be through walking, camping, canoeing, using your senses, looking or sitting quietly, conducting historical or nature surveys, going on or leading a guided walk, making a map, identifying features, keeping a written or image diary, or producing artwork.

Conserving a wild place – Taking some personal responsibility for the conservation and protection of the chosen wild place. This could take the form of some practical action such as research, clean-ups, nature surveys, tree planting, path building, clearing invasive plants, creating trails and habitats, campaigning or taking an interest in related environmental issues.

Sharing your experiences with others – Letting people know about your own experiences by sharing your feelings, thoughts and knowledge. This could be through displays, photo albums, presentations, articles and poems for newsletters, guided walks, discussions or web pages.

There are three progressive levels of the Award – Discovery, Explorer and Conserver. Each should encompass all four challenges but increasing commitment and effort is required with each successive level.

One of the aims of the John Muir Award Scheme is to offer a framework to promote environmental awareness, involvement and responsibility and to promote holistic outdoor experiences that combine:

Heart – promoting strong feelings about a place or about nature, such that people will care about it, want to know more and want to do something to protect it.

Head – developing knowledge and understanding of nature and the value of wilderness, the interdependence of living systems, and the threats to wild places, with the intention that this will encourage a sense of responsibility and stronger feelings.

Hand – getting actively involved and taking practical action for a place; a sense of 'putting something back', that helps people enjoy and value the experience more.

A key idea is that it is possible to start with any one of these above three dimensions which will then lead into the development of the other two, something that would cater for different learning styles in terms of attracting children's initial interest. As it is, with careful and integrated planning it could be used as an ideal vehicle to develop the necessary creative, innovative and radical in-depth fieldwork which could help children open up to new worlds, particularly in terms of their emotional commitment to a place, while still meeting the requirements of the National Curriculum in a challenging and rewarding way.

A member of the Lochaber Area Pupil Support Service noted that by simply spending time in wild places, the John Muir Award Scheme offers an excellent and enjoyable learning opportunity in which to help young people develop many diverse skills and gain a greater sense of nature, inspiring deeper understanding and care, and in particular learning about the natural environment within their own community.

One example of the Award is a bird-watching project undertaken by a Cumbrian school in the conservation area set aside in their own grounds. On a weekly basis over two terms a group of 11 Year 5 students undertook an extended project that involved:

1   An introduction to the JMA and initial visit to the conservation area.

2   Surveying and mapping of the conservation area onto a simple base map.

3   Local visits to gather information and buy bird boxes/bird food.

4   Helping in the construction of bird boxes, feeders and an observation hide.

5   A visit to the school by a member of the RSPB.

6   Detailed collection of data on weather conditions and bird visits and attempts to identify patterns and the processes behind them.

7   Responsibility for escorting Year 1 and Year 2 students around the site and explaining the project to them.

8   Completion of an individual diary that drew conclusions together at the end.

The project was integrated into the school timetable and allowed scope for varied research work by small groups of students on a regular weekly basis, as well as opportunities for self-discovery, taking personal responsibility and applying the learning beyond school to home and wider world.

www.johnmuiraward.org

Forest Schools

Forest Schools is a concept that originated in Denmark in the 1950s as a way of teaching about and developing a more respectful and balanced connection with the natural world. By the 1980s it had been integrated into the Danish Early Years programme and since the mid-1990s Forest Schools, and the ethos behind them, have been spreading throughout England and Wales.

Forest Schools are aimed to be 'an innovative approach to outdoor play and learning' at both Key Stages 1 and 2 and beyond, which encourages and inspires individuals to develop their own understanding of the world through their participation in small, achievable tasks in a familiar local woodland environment: a 'classroom without walls'. By focusing on the underlying process and immersing children in the environment, the intention of the programmed activities is to provide a vehicle for all round personal development and discovery about self, others and the natural environment. These programmes are designed to be fun and informative, developing a sense of freedom and adventure by allowing students to explore environments experientially through play, while incorporating methods of accelerated learning and encouraging a responsible approach to the management of risk.

Throughout what is normally a ten-week Forest School programme, a key element is that a very similar structure is used for each session, although the theme or content varies from week to week. This helps pupils make connections to their previous learning and experiences and initially enables them to feel more comfortable with the learning environment. Advantages of this programme are the opportunities for children to learn 'from' the environment, as well as 'about', 'in' or 'for' it, as has traditionally been the case, and for them to develop affection for, and understanding of, what becomes a 'place of their own'.

www.forestschools.com

The Outdoor School

The Outdoor School originated with a small cluster of primary schools in Roseland, Cornwall, in 2004, and was set up initially to take Key Stage 1 pupils into the outdoors to learn. The primary aim was to 'make a difference' by enthusing children and providing them with the opportunity to develop a sense of adventure, while at the same time recognising that it was possible to teach a large proportion of the Key Stage 1 pupils outdoors, given a suitable local area in which to do so.

The nine primary schools in the area used this opportunity to experience a different way of learning in the great outdoors, and the Outdoor School now has two spheres: 'Call of the Wild', which is off-site, and 'Outdoor Learning', which is based within the school grounds. Both involve a variety of sensory and practical activities around an evolving curriculum that encourages discovery, questioning, exploration and the inspiration to love the 'outdoors'.

To overcome the 'fear of the unknown' and anxieties over health and safety, training days were held for staff and taster sessions for parents so that they could become familiar with the chosen 'outdoor classroom'. According to one Reception/Year 1 teacher, the outcome has been a revelation, and she notes how the children are 'learning on their own initiative – it's almost self-generating . . . It's allowed me to see ways of teaching you don't learn in college, and given me the confidence to try things outdoors. In class, children do things that are all so structural, but nothing on their own' (Mourant 2005).

The Outdoor School offers immense scope for cross-curricular activity and for teachers to deliver the curriculum more creatively, helped by the fact that the children are in a place where they have much more freedom to discover and be themselves.

www.outdoorschool.co.uk

Going Global in the Outdoors

A 'Survival Pack for Future Citizens: Global Issues and Sustainable Development', Going Global in the Outdoors incorporates several projects being co-ordinated and disseminated nationally by Cumbria Development Education Centre, and extending to include Key Stages 1 and 2 and special needs. This particular full or half day programme is targeted at Key Stage 2 and is focused on developing children's understanding of the concept of 'needs and wants' through the use of the outdoor environment. It uses activities in the local area (which can be adapted for the school grounds) as a means to introduce children to the things we need to survive, such as water, food and shelter, but goes on to illustrate that for these to be met now and in the future we also need to focus on sustainable development issues on both the local and global scale. It makes use of a combination of direct practical experience along with the techniques of 'philosophy for children' and 'critical skills' to encourage the development of the feeling and thinking necessary to help children recognise the relationship between themselves and their environment and how, as an individual, they can make a difference.

> 'I feel it is important to relate the activities to real-life situations. This gives credibility to the learning process and enables children to see the relevance of these issues in their own lives. The natural learning environment reinforces the experience and makes it enjoyable for everyone involved.'
>
> (Cumbrian teacher)

www.cdec.org.uk

What would an ideal framework be like?

The key characteristics of each of these potential frameworks is the opportunity they create for active multifaceted open-ended enquiry in relation to a specific local place;

in a context with which the children can become familiar and learn to develop both love and understanding of themselves, each other and their world.

As Swift and Lambert (2005) note, 'the local scale of experience provides certain kinds of insights, stories and understanding', and ideally any such local place-based framework should also open up the opportunity of expanding this understanding to the global scale, and perhaps most importantly, acknowledge their interdependence. The phrase 'Act locally, think globally' then begins to take on some significance.

Can we establish frameworks of our own that will work in our specific situations? And to what extent are we, as teachers, part of the problem rather than the solution?

What action do we need to take?

What barriers do we face?

There are enormous barriers to achieving such development and the whole prospect of doing so can seem a daunting challenge, but do we have any real option in the long term? No one is suggesting that it is going to be easy, but then anything that is worth something usually never is. So where do we go from here?

There is clear evidence of the inherent value of fieldwork as it stands now. This is illustrated, for example, by the House of Commons Education and Skills Select Committee Report (2005) which referred to of the powerful impact that out-of-classroom learning has on young people, and the Teacher Training Agency's (now the Training and Development Agency) *Handbook of Guidance* (2005: 32) which notes that 'valuable pupil learning can take place in a wide range of out-of-school contexts [and that] teachers need to be able to plan to make the best use of these opportunities for learning, and recognise the additional value that they bring'.

The significance of fieldwork is even greater in light of the need to develop those aspects essential to a 'sustainable' Way of Being and yet, as Rita Gardner, Director of the Royal Geographical Society notes, we are faced with a 'profound decline in opportunities for fieldwork and outdoor education' (Slater 2005). The reasons are many-fold but it is imperative that we seek ways and means to overcome these as a matter of urgency.

At government level, the House of Commons Education and Skills Select Committee Report (2005), which described outdoor learning as extremely patchy and stated that not enough had been done to publicise the benefits, called for a £30 million investment in:

A DfES 'Manifesto for Outdoor Learning' which is to contain a commitment to give all children the right/opportunity to take part in 'a wide range of high quality outdoor learning, including at least one residential experience as part of the school curriculum'.

A national Outdoor Champion.

Ring-fenced funding to promote outdoor education with the money being targeted at schools in deprived areas.

Measures to reduce paperwork that school trip leaders are expected to complete.

Professional development opportunities for teachers.

At the local level, one of the most significant problems recognised in the Report is that many schools are deterred by the false perception that a high degree of risk attaches to outdoor education, and that teachers' fears over legal action if things go wrong on school trips are 'out of all proportion' to the risks.

High profile tragedies have made schools wary of taking pupils on trips, and fear of litigation and accusations against teachers have prompted the NASUWT to advise its members not to take part in trips on the grounds that 'society no longer appears to accept the concept of a genuine accident'.

So what about risk? – keeping it in perspective

Risk can be defined as 'incurring the chance of unfortunate consequences by doing something', and as such is an inherent part of life. Sometimes we deliberately seek risk, most of the time we seek to avoid it, but it is when taking risks, emotionally, physically, socially, intellectually, that we are most alive and open to intense learning experiences. Adventurers and entrepreneurs take risks all the time, on the assumption that the rewards will outweigh the costs, and we need future generations who are willing and responsible enough to do the same.

However, we are currently in danger of trying to protect ourselves from risk completely, rather than creating opportunities for children to experience, and manage, it. Looking to the long term, is that the sort of strategy that will create citizens willing to take on the challenges of a new sustainable way of life?

Risks – the facts

Several facts highlighted by the Education and Skills Select Committee Report are that;

- In England in 2003 there were an estimated 7–10 million days of school visits and only one fatality.
- There have been 57 fatal accidents on school trips over the 19 years from May 1986 to June 2004, involving adults and children, of which 13 were in one minibus crash. This averages three fatalities a year, a high proportion of which were road traffic accidents.
- On average young people (aged between 5 and 19) are over 200 times more likely to be killed in a road traffic accident and over 30 times more likely to be killed as a result of accidents in the home than they are on a school visit.

Risks – the myths

Media exaggeration of the 'compensation culture' is generally exactly that and a recent report by the independent advisory group the Better Regulation Task Force (2004) actually found that there is no reason to believe such a culture. In fact the number of accident claims in the UK was almost constant between the years 2000 and 2003, and even went down in 2004.

Likewise, contrary to public perception, it does not appear as if judges wish to see the UK turn into a 'nanny state' either. A good example of judicial attitude to risk is the case of John Peter Thomlinson versus Congleton Borough Council and Cheshire County Council in the House of Lords in 2003. One of the judges made the following comment:

> it is not, and should never be, the policy of the law to require the protection of the foolhardy or reckless few to deprive, or interfere with, the enjoyment by the remainder of society of the liberties and amenities to which they are rightly entitled. Does the law require that all trees be cut down because some youths may climb them and fall? Does the law require the coastline and other beauty spots to be lined with warning notices. The answer to all these questions is, of course, no.
>
> (McDonald 2005)

How might we overcome them?

Ultimately then, it is up to the individual schools and teachers who value fieldwork and outdoor learning to ensure that it continues; so what practical steps can teachers take?

The government is to issue new 'Guidelines on Outings' to ensure that staff who take reasonable care and follow guidelines are protected by law from being sued in the event of an accident, and to help LAs cut paperwork and bureaucracy, without compromising safety. The guidelines will recommend that schools use generic risk assessment forms (which help confirm adherence to the guidelines) and that LAs take out one insurance policy for their schools that covers all liabilities relating to trips.

As long as teachers follow recognised guidelines, such as those provided in the *Health and Safety of Pupils on Educational Visits: A Good Practice Guide* (DfES 1998), which includes model forms for parental consent and risk assessment, and can show they have done so, there is little to fear and much of immense value to be gained.

Key points to consider

1 Make use of your LA Outdoor Education Adviser and School Educational Visits Co-ordinator.

2 Plan thoroughly and try to foresee and pre-empt any potential problems.

3 Do a pre-visit if at all possible, for your own peace of mind if nothing else.

4 Complete a risk assessment for your own benefit and as legal back up for the school.

5 Ensure you have a standby plan and conform with any emergency procedures.

Extending frontiers . . . and . . . opening up to a new world?

The journey to a new 'sustainable' Way of Being will be a challenging one, and we need future generations who are prepared and able to rise to that challenge. Wherever the new frontiers of the map of the future might be, we need to help children experience the thrill of being 'out on the edge', where how they feel, think and act meets uncharted and mysterious territory, and where the only way through is by life-enhancing enquiry towards a sense of our wholeness with ourselves and our earthly home, and beyond that to a Way of Being of which we as yet know nothing at all. What is the role that geography fieldwork has to play in that? – It's up to you . . .

Acknowlegements

Michelle Donoghue and Jonathan Walkingshaw, The John Muir Award Scheme – Cumbria.
Norma Bagot and Clare Reagan, Fell View Primary School.
John Nixon and Alison Boyd, Moor Row Primary School.
Tim Coleman and Alison Wild, Tebay Community School.
Laura Watson, Lowther Endowed Primary School.
Ruth Suddaby, Greystoke Primary School.
Catherine Mole, Forest Schools/Cumbria Wildlife Trust.
Danielle Metcalfe and Heather Troughton, St Martin's College.
Jayne Buchanan, United Utilities.
Gina Mullarkey, Cumbria Development Education Centre.
Kate Jordan, Grizedale Forest Education Service.
Adrian Letts, George Romney School.
Tania Crockett, Grizedale Forest Education Service.

References

Better Regulation Task Force (2004) *Report: 'Better Routes to Redress'*, May. London: Better Regulation Task Force.

DfES (1998) *Health and Safety of Pupils on Educational Visits: A Good Practice Guide*. London: DfES.

House of Commons (2005) *Education and Skills Select Committee Report: 'Education outside the Classroom', Second Report, February 2005*. London: The Stationery Office.

John Muir Award (2001) *John Muir Award Information Handbook*. Edinburgh: John Muir Award.

Lambert, D. (2005) 'An axis to grind', *Times Educational Supplement*, 4 March.

Louv, R. (2005) *Last Child in the Woods*. Chapel Hill: Algonquin Books.

McDonald, A. (2005) 'Fell running and litigation', *Fellrunner Magazine*, June edition, Stockport Fell Running Association.

Mourant, A. (2005) 'Lesson "al fresco" ', *Times Educational Supplement*, 13 May.

Orr, D. W. (1994) *Earth in Mind*. Washington DC: Island Press.

Osbourne, J. (2005) 'Build your own bridges', *Times Educational Supplement*, 7 January.

Rawling, E. (2005) 'New found land', *Times Educational Supplement*, 4 February.

Slater, J. (2005) 'MPs angry over school trip fear', *Times Educational Supplement*, 11 February.

Sterling, S. (2001) *Sustainable Education*. Totnes: Green Books.

Swift, D. and Lambert, D. (2005) 'Swept up together', *Times Educational Supplement*, 4 February.

Teacher Training Agency (2005) *Handbook of Guidance*. London: Teacher Training Agency.

Web links

CDEC (2003) A Survival Pack for Future Citizens

www.teachernet.gov.uk/wholeschool/healthandsafety/visits
Includes 'Health and Safety of Pupils on Educational Visits: A Good Practice Guide', plus supplements on
- 'Standards for LEAs in Overseeing Educational Visits'
- 'Standards for Adventure'
- 'A Handbook for Group Leaders'
- 'Group Safety at Water Margins'

www.teachernet.gov.uk/emergencies/planning/educationalvisits
Includes 'Educational Visits – Model Forms'

www.hse.gov.uk/schooltrips   general information on school trips

www.hse.gov.uk/pubns/   risk assessment

www.teacherline.org.uk   school trips

How can children connect to a distant place through drama?

Nigel Toye and Denise Evans

Why use drama?

HOW DO WE teach children anything? One of the key issues is whether we can interest them enough to engage with the material. It is really not sufficient to put the material in front of them and expect them to learn from it. Research tells us that if children experience material in an active way then they remember it more purposefully (Cooper and McIntyre 1995; Beard and Wilson 2002; Moon 2004). Therefore one of the challenges for us teaching geography is how we manoeuvre children into an interactive relationship with material and ideas relating to the learning objective, such as 'a distant place'? This is the focus of this chapter.

One of the problems is in the idea of 'distance'. There are implications of irrelevance, strangeness and possibly a lack of any previous understanding. One of the most common approaches to teaching this area of geography is to get the children to compare the distant place with the place they already know, the place where they live. This raises other questions.

The approach is based on an adult view of learning, embodying a number of assumptions. Do children really know their own place? Is the local knowledge attractive and interesting to them? Will studying their locale guarantee a positive connection to the new place? Can we really make meaningful connections between the two places as far as the children are concerned? We have material on the spot for the local environment, but the evidence of the distant place is not going to be immediate, and cannot be visited; it is going to be only words and pictures, a contrast which reinforces that distance. In fact one pupil, when asked about other approaches to teaching the topic dismissed it as 'just pictures'.

We know from experience of using drama to teach a range of subjects that through drama we can create a situation and a person within a fictional setting to embody ideas for the learning focus, in this case the distant place, Kenya. Children make their learning connections best through specific people with whom to interact and have a relationship. This was borne out at the school which used the drama as the stimulus for their work on Kenya. When interviewed and asked what they most remembered so far, they talked about the drama and the visitor who had spent time teaching and living in Kenya.

It is important to state at this stage that we do not claim to use drama to teach all aspects of a geography topic. But it provides an interesting context which children can directly engage with and help to create. They have some ownership of the teaching and learning situation and this motivates them.

We aim to use, within the drama, a range of the sources of information which are commonly used: maps, artefacts, an account by a person from a distant place (albeit fictional), photographs of the locality and a resource pack and books as summarised by Weldon (2004: 207). We would also claim that using these different types of resources together, within a created context, makes it easier to teach about distant places. The work is focused on children's current understandings because we create a child with whom they can identify. The artefacts have meaning for the role and therefore carry significance, in a geographical sense.

What is drama?

'When doing drama you learn in a fun way. You basically have a game, really, but it's like you're learning as well' (Emma, Hornby School). As Emma demonstrates, children seem to instinctively understand what drama is and how it works. They recognise the fictional world of story and how to play within it. As teachers using drama, we provide that fictional context, but need to identify the learning we aim to engender.

The use of a fictional role, in a fictional situation, can be the focus of key objections to this mode of working, on both geography and history. There is the likelihood of some distortion of the facts, of the 'truth'. We need to be very aware of this and to make sure that the role has a firm basis in fact, that there is good research and knowledge to support the created situation. However, are other methods of presenting children with a distant place more grounded in the facts and less open to distortion? If you present the children with photographs, we would maintain you are still asking for a massive leap of imagination on the part of the children. One pack we have used shows Kenyan children at their desks in a bare classroom. The interpretation of this by children in this country could easily be that the Kenyans are very disadvantaged and less able than they are, a problematical stereotype. What is missing is the sense that the Kenyan children could be said to have a massive advantage in that they generally value their education much more than children in this country. Likewise, a photograph of children walking to their school could be interpreted as

Kenyans having no cars or public transport. The missing, opposing idea, is that these children are less polluting in their lifestyle and much healthier. Thus the imaginative demand of photographs, which have to be interpreted, can easily be seen as akin to the fictional approach and yet lacks the first-hand dialogue and creation of context that drama can give. With the photographs, how do teachers structure the children's responses in a positive way, something the drama structure sets out to do?

What are we talking about when referring to 'drama'?

Drama is both a subject in its own right and a powerful teaching and learning method. When using drama in education with primary aged children, it can be viewed as an alternative approach to learning. How does this happen? Firstly, drama requires a well-structured lesson plan which outlines the process, identifies the learning objectives and considers the drama strategies to be employed. Our lesson plan focused upon learning objectives which can be summarised by the Key Stage 2 requirements identified in developing a global dimension in the school curriculum.

> Pupils develop their understanding beyond their own experience and build up their knowledge of the wider world and of different societies and cultures. They learn about the similarities and differences between people and places around the world and about disparities in the world. They develop their sense of social justice and moral responsibility and begin to understand that their own choices can affect global issues as well as local ones.
>
> (DfEE 2000: 6)

Further exploration of the relationship between drama and geography will be looked at later in this chapter.

Drama strategies

Drama strategies which were used in our lesson included tableaux, thought tracking, hot seating, forum theatre and, most importantly, teacher in role (TiR). Tableaux involve the children working in groups to create a still image, photograph-like, of a significant moment. Thought tracking arises naturally from tableaux. Children holding their still image can be asked to reveal what their 'character' is thinking at that precise moment. Hot seating is a useful way of questioning a character (which may be the TiR), to find out what further information is required in order to proceed with the drama.

Forum theatre involves the children in collectively speaking as one character. When working towards helping a character, forum utilise their ideas as they argue on his or her behalf. Central to the drama lesson is the teacher in role, which requires a teacher to take on the role of a character in the drama. Through the role a teacher can challenge, affirm, encourage and examine the children's learning. Careful choice of the type of role will determine how children may engage with the learning. For example, a 'needy' role will require knowledge and expertise from the children; a 'misguided' role will encourage children to be instructive and caring; an authoritative role (similar to the traditional teacher role) may serve as a useful role for maintaining the order of the lesson and a reminder of the learning objectives.

The drama session Emma referred to was inspired by a story, *The Sandal* (Bradman 1989). This story focuses upon how an ancient Roman sandal found in the present can provide an opportunity for children to discover the past. Developing this idea, we devised a drama where an artefact from Kenya becomes unexpectedly reunited with its owner. The geographical focus of Kenya was chosen to introduce a topic which one of the schools we were working with planned to study. The two main characters we would be presenting as teacher in role were Mrs Brown, the exhibition organiser, and Kilesi, a Kenyan boy of Maasai heritage. Mrs Brown's role was 'authoritative' and served to contextualise the drama and provide information when required. Kilesi's role could be regarded as 'needy', thus inspiring the children to learn about him and his culture in order to help him. The roles are well matched to empowering the children's attainment of the geographical enquiry and skills set out in the National Curriculum (DfEE/QCA 1999). For example, asking geographical questions, identifying and explaining different views that people hold about geographical issues and communicating these appropriately, are integrated into the teacher in role's interaction with the class. There were two of us to take the three TiR roles in the drama – the exhibition organiser, Kilesi, the Maasai boy, and Mr Torrance, the owner of the key object – but one teacher can take all of these roles and the children take over the boy role later. While it is not possible to give the full lesson plan, the following is a narrative outline of the drama in three main stages.

Outline of the drama

The first stage – building belief in the drama

To ascertain what information children already held about Kenya, we began with setting up the context of an exhibition celebrating Kenya. In order to build their belief in the situation children worked in groups to identify what would be found in each of their displays.

Moving more into drama mode, groups shared this information with the class by creating tableaux, which portrayed themselves observing their own exhibits. The observing class teacher later identified how opportunities to discuss cultural differences arose during this part of the lesson.

The second stage – presenting the problem for the children to solve

Once the exhibition was established, TiR as the exhibition organiser presented them with a key exhibit, a wooden figurine of a Maasai warrior under a plastic cover with signs warning of an alarm if disturbed. With the artefact in place, narration led the children, in role as the exhibition workers, to unexpectedly meet TiR as Kilesi, the Kenyan boy, bringing him to the children in a fictional way.

The children discovered that Kilesi had sold, by mistake, a wooden figurine back in Kenya and was in trouble as a result. They made the connection with the artefact in their exhibition, now owned by a Mr Torrance. Kilesi appealed to them to give the figurine back.

The third stage – investigating and resolving the problem

Following on from this point of interaction between the children and the TiR, the content varied. However, the direction of the learning remained consistently focused upon the dilemma of reconciling the boy's need to obtain the figurine and return home with it and the owner's right to possess the figurine, which he had kindly lent for the exhibition. Later the class teacher remarked that at this point the children were making further comparisons with Britain, another geographical skill.

Through using drama we presented a particular structure for learning:

- we devised a fictional context (the exhibition);
- we provided a shared dilemma (how to help the boy and the present owner of the artefact);
- the dilemma encouraged investigation and analysis (questioning the boy, gathering facts and information);
- this led to the opportunity to affect the outcome (persuading the owner to give the figurine back).

The structure is defined by the teacher, but it requires children to contribute to the content and develop it. In order to incorporate their contributions, the teacher must listen carefully to what children are saying. But what are we listening for? In drama, listening to children is the key, not just listening for the 'right' answer as often happens in other teaching situations, but listening for ideas which can influence the forming of solutions and compromises which affect the outcome of the story. During the drama, we can encourage children's responses in and out of role. The TiR has responsibility for the learning as any teacher has. However, she is able to facilitate the learning by interacting directly with the children in role, operating within the drama, providing challenges which develop and extend children's thinking.

Drama in action

Our starting question for this project was, 'Can we show that children respond usefully to a stimulus created through drama?' The settings for using the drama detailed above were two very different schools, both geographically and demographically:

Broad Oak, a large urban school in Manchester, and Hornby St Margaret's, a small, rural school near Lancaster. In the former, we worked with a Year 4 class consisting of 15 boys and 11 girls, with an ethnic mix of six of Pakistani heritage, three of mixed race (Pakistani/English), one of Indian heritage, two of Middle Eastern heritage, two of Bangladeshi heritage and the rest white British. There were no African or Caribbean heritage children in either class. The class at Hornby was all white British, a Key Stage 2 class made up of 12 Year 4 children and four Year 3 children. There were eight boys and eight girls. Neither class had studied Kenya before and the rural school was using our input as the starting point for such a study. The urban school had completed a study of Pakistan and therefore were not going to develop the work on Kenya any further.

Initially we developed the hypothesis that we might discover major differences in the responses of the two classes to the drama. We thought that the class that had already done a distance place study might respond in some ways influenced by that study, that they, being more ethnically mixed, might have a more varied set of expectations of the place. Our stereotypical view of the rural school, where all the children were very local to the village, was that it might be much narrower in outlook and that that might influence the children's responses. It transpired, as you will see below, that the children's responses were not significantly different, and the study became much more about how the drama was received by both classes.

The geography focus

For the two classes we worked with, the geography curriculum was focused upon the theme, 'A Contrasting Locality Overseas'. Weldon (2004) offers a number of reasons for studying other places with young people, some of which become more meaningful when considering them in the light of our drama practice. For example, drama 'uses and develops their interest and natural curiosity about places' (this may seem obvious but what stimulates the children to be interested in the first place?). Learning about a place through the interaction with TiR not only provides stimulus but also, as Weldon says, 'provides opportunities for them to explore ideas and skills'.

Through interacting with TiR as Kilesi, the class were confronted with a dilemma which engaged their developing knowledge of Kenya and utilised their universal understanding of what it is to be a child with a problem. This manifested itself in the pupils being involved in high quality discussion and debate surrounding Kilesi's dilemma.

To deal with this they had been placed in the position of knowledge and therefore power. TiR as Kilesi was placed in the opposite position; he was not from England, he did not know what to do about his problem. Consequently the children were motivated and empowered to learn about Kilesi's country. They were in a perfect position to 'value diversity in places, environments and cultures', again to quote Weldon.

Geography and children's responses to the drama 'The Maasai Boy'

The QCA guidelines (2000) for questions about 'A Contrasting Locality Overseas' follow a compatible outline with our drama lesson plan so we can see how the children's input works to address the following questions.

Where is the locality?

The question of Kenya's location was examined in our initial introduction when considering setting up the fictional exhibition. To help children to learn about another place we must acknowledge the place where they are. We used maps of the world and Kenya to let the children show what they knew of the locations. We must also recognise what children already know; we do not need to treat pupils as deficit learners. In our drama the pupils were placed in their own country, setting up the fictional exhibition, which not only utilised their existing knowledge of Kenya but provided the opportunity to make sense of it. Consider responses from two Broad Oak children when discussing how 'our country is different from his (Kilesi's) country'. Sandy explained, 'We can get water from a tap and they have to walk a long way for about two hours to get some water and sometimes it's not that clean.' To which Sean replied, 'My Dad was telling me in the 1800s England was like that and all the scientists said it was because of the water.'

What is the locality like?

The guidelines (QCA 2000) suggest using pictures to be drawn and labelled, which connects to our group work of identifying and labelling what would be included in the exhibition. Both classes of children were uncertain of the situation at the beginning and needed to be made comfortable before they contributed more spontaneously. Of course, we are not using drama techniques at this point, just discussing their expectations of Africa. It was important to get them thinking about their own ideas before the main diagnostic stage about Africa.

The Hornby (rural) class were slow at the discussion stage. The following note was made immediately after the session.

The initial discussion of what might be in the exhibition produced a range of answers very slowly. Amy's suggestion was the most advanced: 'African traditions'; however she saw this as 'sacrificing and rain dance'. The other observations about Africa from different children were: 'hot country – lions, tigers – giraffes – monkeys – that people suffered lack of food and water – they make clothes out of dead animals – there is poaching of elephant tusks for ivory – hotels – bones – tribe weapons – cannon, guns and armour which was modified to knife, spears, slingshot when challenged over the problem of the heat'. Gradually we began to build a picture but we had to work very hard at this.

In the early discussion of the exhibition, Broad Oak (urban) children were quicker in response but offered similar sorts of ideas and produced:

fruit trees – fossils – stuffed cheetah – people drumming – pictures of what they wear (straw dresses) – picture of people in the desert – a model boat – elephants – monkeys – pottery and plants, with patterns on the pots – dinosaurs and cavemen (a contribution that was criticised by another member of the class as being archaeologically impossible).

We can see here some standard stereotypes and some problems of perception. The belief-building section of the drama, when the children were establishing the exhibition, was done with some confidence, but of course involved a number of generalisations and misconceptions, as the lists above show.

The Broad Oak children, when we tracked their thoughts as people looking at their imagined exhibits, created interesting detail:

Frog pond with tadpoles – dart shape on frog – Tropical – Straw – Fossils – Cave – Dolphins – Four elephants, a mum and dad and two children – Palm tree on a beach.
Cheetahs defending cubs – Dinosaurs eating caveman – An elephant with a lion there.
Fossils – A skeleton – Skins worn in the past – Bones and a model in the same position showing what it looked like.
Fruit, sticky and woolly – A blue plant with spiky pointy leaves – haven't seen a plant like that before – Palm trees big and hairy – Taking a picture of a wild boar.
Snakes in covered containers.

The children felt considerable ownership of what they were doing and this could be seen as a negative thing if they were to hold onto those initial expectations, but we have evidence that by the end of the drama they were able to talk about and let go of the more dubious suggestions. For example, both classes included a tiger in the exhibition and later we pointed out that there are no tigers in Africa. Neither class had any problem in accepting this correction and one girl at Hornby volunteered in the debrief interviews, six weeks after the drama, that she had been interested to learn this fact. Also at Hornby they were able to laugh at their own ideas of the African traditions of the sacrifice and the rain dance, and accept that they needed to find evidence to substantiate them, but that they were unlikely to be the truth.

The main challenge to the stereotypes during the drama is the use of the teacher in role as Kilesi, who can present other views and other ideas. We cannot ignore that there are common misconceptions, coming from a variety of sources. The children will bring these to the session.

What might it be like to live in the locality?

This question was directly addressed when meeting TiR as Kilesi, who talked about his life in his home country. He presented them with a more particular and dynamic 'truth' about Kenya because the role (teacher in role) that they met embodied useful information. The key motivation for the children was the fact that this was a boy in trouble with his father because of making a mistake, the selling of the Maasai warrior figurine. The children could identify with his problem, something which is human and not specifically British or Kenyan, a cross-cultural contact point. In this way they got drawn into the situation.

The effect of Kilesi's arrival, TiR, was electric in both the schools. There was suddenly the injection of tension into the situation and children paid attention in a way they had not done before. In the debrief, at Broad Oak, a week after the drama, Chloe picked out this moment to typify what she liked about working in drama, 'It got really exciting ... At the beginning I thought it was going to be just about exhibitions, then a boy suddenly just turned up and we didn't know how he got there.' It is significant that the 'just about exhibitions' response reveals how this child feels about the set up work which is most like an ordinary geography discussion.

The drama took off at this point in both schools because of the tension generated by the sudden appearance of the TiR as the boy. For example, as soon as Kilesi uttered two Kiswahili words, Colin, one of the Broad Oak children, immediately took the initiative. He said 'Do you speak Maasai?' and was thus accepting the geographical context, albeit he did not know the name for the language at this point.

The teacher, as Kilesi, was able to input ideas about Kenya – for example, the Maasai as a cattle-keeping people; the climate of Kenya, when he talked about the rainy season and the plentiful grass; and the fact that Kilesi goes to school. All of this information was eased into the drama as he talked to the children about himself and his problem.

Both sets of children accepted the role-play and took risks in engaging with solving the problem. At Broad Oak they even helped Kilesi himself to get a perspective on what the warrior figurine represented. When they discovered he did not like the way it portrayed his people as savages, Chloe replied, 'but people are coming to the exhibition to look at that. They find it really interesting – they don't think you're like that – that you're a savage.' This girl revealed a sophisticated awareness of another cultural heritage, arising in the drama and modelled for the other children looking on. Colin added 'they learn about the history of Kenya, the animals of Kenya. There was a special find of fossils in Kenya.'

Having met Kilesi, the children in both schools realised they had to raise the problem with Mrs Brown, the organiser. At Broad Oak we had sudden activity from the group; some of them went off to bring her over and were telling her what had happened; at the same time others were reassuring Kilesi and asking him for more background. There was a very productive confusion at this point, with many conversations at once, so we stopped the drama to discuss the situation out of role (OoR) and decide on the best way forward, thus focusing the thinking.

Ideas can be introduced at points and questions raised by the children. Using an artefact is very helpful and when Mustafa from Broad Oak referred to the lamp that Kilesi was carrying, Kilesi was able to talk about the lamp having been made from tins, one of which contained insecticide to kill mosquitoes. He then passionately informed them about the malaria. 'My brother suffers from it.' He told them how it recurs every year. 'You see that is much more what life is like in our country than warriors with spears.' The quality of listening was very high as Kilesi explained the relevance of the tin oil lamp and its connection to mosquitoes and malaria. Because the children were engaged with the role they paid attention to this so that at the end of the drama they adopted the ideas. When they appealed to the owner of the wooden figurine they were talking passionately about substituting the lamp as an exhibit, telling him that the oil can was a truer representation of Kenya today, 'because it shows what they can do and what they have to deal with, the malaria' and 'it [the can] has lots of stories'.

We can see that in both schools the children identified with Kilesi and supported him, to the extent that they wanted to make sure that he achieved his goal of getting the figurine back. At Hornby they urged, 'He really needs it back', Isla adding, 'It's his father's father's father's!' This example, taken from the children's experience in the drama, shows how they are able to 'combat ignorance, partiality and bias, thus helping to avoid stereotyping and the development of prejudice' (Weldon 2004).

In addition to the lamp and warrior figurine, we used other objects from Kenya, typical of resources available from Development Education Centres throughout the country, to help build the context. By the end of their drama the children under-stood what they meant for the Maasai people and for the drama. At Broad Oak a photograph is requested by Mr Torrance to show Kilesi, with the warrior figurine, lamp and the toy motorbike (also made out of recycled materials), posing with the exhibition advisers. When Ricky is chosen to be Kilesi, Isaac is heard to say to him as he holds the motorbike, 'You are SO lucky'.

Pupils' reflections on the locality

Ask pupils to reflect on how their ideas regarding the locality have changed and developed. What other questions might they ask? The interviews we held with a sample of children at a later date show their enthusiasm and interest. They were clear in both schools that they would change and add material to an exhibition as their perspective had changed now. They wanted to add things from the drama, for example the oil lamp, but also more models and pictures. Mustafa suggested, 'portraits of famous people in the past, clothes, what the landscape is and what things are used in Kenya'.

Now the children were eager for further research. The Hornby children had already carried on the project with their own teacher by the time we interviewed them, six weeks later. They said they would now add ideas they had learned since the drama – 'a map with the Rift Valley on it', 'The Game Park and what's there'.

Responses to the drama showed how well the children remembered it. At Hornby, Lee was very clear about why drama works for him, aware of its combination of fiction and fact, 'It is real . . . some of it can't happen in real life (like Kilesi just appearing) . . . some of it can be real life.' They showed how the teacher picked up on points from the drama: 'Mrs T put up the [Kiswahili] words Kilesi said and we practised saying them.' They were very sure that the drama helped their learning, but Emma suggested the drama might be more useful at the end of the project.

At Broad Oak, the question of how they viewed Kilesi brought this response from Aneela: 'A normal boy that is very kind and honest and always likes to be happy and help people.' When asked why she thought he was honest, Aneela replied: 'Because he wants everything to become normal and he does.' The children then went on to consider what Kilesi might have thought others were thinking about him. Sean said, 'He thought that some people would make fun of his people and country because of the clothes the Maasai warrior wore.' When asked why he would worry about that, Sandy said, 'Because he's not like everyone else. He's different.' Through their communication with TiR as Kilesi the class were able to build positive attitudes towards other people around the world.

The inclusive nature of drama

In the execution of this drama we saw very clearly how advantageous it was for inclusion of all the children. Because drama differentiates by outcome rather than by task, the children can access it as they see it and as they feel comfortable. They are not under any individual pressure.

We want to instance four children with significant problems of different sorts in the two classes. All of them were seen to benefit by their teachers, some of them very considerably. Isaac was described as a refusenik by his teacher. In the normal class situation he would refuse to do things. He was not aggressive but silent in his response and could be very difficult. The teacher and class assistant stated later that at the beginning of the morning they would have bet that Isaac would not have coped and would have left the hall. In the event, he stayed for the duration of the drama, even if at times he was peripheral. He watched very closely.

There were signs, reviewing the video, that he might have been attracted towards upsetting the drama at some points. He was clearly hanging around the figurine on its plinth and the teachers observed that it would have been typical behaviour if he had knocked the plinth and figurine over. He clearly chose not to do that. Why did he participate in this way and not reject the work? Of course, he was able to be one of the crowd without being under pressure to do anything in particular and either he was properly interested or the very positive ethos generated by the rest of the children held him in check without any teacher intervention. The result of this was that he took part in the educational experience for the whole of the morning and did not have to be separated out.

Colin in contrast got very involved in the drama. He was defined equally socially inept in the classroom, being bright, but not liking to show his intelligence in front of the others. Instead, in a normal lesson he would often wait till the end and then seek the undivided attention of the teacher on his own. Unfortunately, in trying to speak to her he can stammer for fully ten minutes with the pressure of trying to get out what he wants to say. When we were told after the drama that Colin had this problem, we couldn't believe it. He had been instrumental in helping to lead the drama and never once stammered.

If Colin does get the teacher's attention in class he tends to monopolise it. But in the drama, when he adopted the role of Kilesi in the forum theatre and had come to the end of what he wanted to say, he turned to the next person saying, 'I am handing over to another Kilesi now', showing an unusual concern for others. Thus we can say that Colin, in the comfort of the fiction, is able to behave as a member of the class and at the same time use his considerable abilities.

Ricky is normally a very difficult child in class. He will avoid work and cause trouble. During the drama he behaved impeccably and contributed. He had, as his reward at the end, the opportunity to stand as Kilesi in the final photograph. As he left the drama he was heard to ask his teacher, 'Was I good?', to which his teacher was able to reply, 'You were very good'.

Gregory, has a statement of special educational needs and works with a support teacher. He has gradually been overcoming his tendency to sit, covering his face with his hands, when he cannot do things. He was not observed to do very much in the drama except to follow when the class was working as a large group and then participate in small-group work with the help of the other children. His teacher was very pleased that he was there listening and paying attention for the whole morning.

Finally, drama can give space for children who do not want to be too active in their contributions. In Broad Oak some of the girls of Asian heritage did not say or do anything noticeable when the class was operating as a large group. However, it is clear from the video that they are able to be part of the small-group process in setting up the exhibition. Their teacher explained that, usually, if they have ideas they look for someone else to articulate them rather than speak out themselves.

The saving grace of our style of drama is that no one is pushed to speak out, something that their teacher, herself of Asian heritage, was worried would be the case. We allow for different styles and different personalities. We apply a model but it is flexible and responsive to how the children want to operate. So these girls could be quiet and supportive without feeling any pressure.

We would suggest that this lack of pressure is very important for children in the primary age range. On other occasions we have found that even quiet children, when they get used to drama, can find a voice. They need to be given time to do that, to build their confidence.

Teacher response

The drama session was viewed from different perspectives by the two class teachers. In the Hornby school the session would start the topic on Kenya. In the Manchester school it was an isolated drama, with a retrospective view as to how it may have been used for the topic on Pakistan. When interviewing the teachers after the drama session, the Hornby teacher, Mrs T, would speak from a position of what she would actually do as a consequence of the drama input and the Manchester teacher, Mrs J, would contemplate its potential for future application. In addition, both teachers would examine its impact on the individual pupils in their classes and the wider curriculum implications.

During the drama, Mrs T was able to recognise pupils' initial perceptions of Kenya. She identified a substantial amount of stereotypical misunderstanding about modern-day Kenya. Mrs T expressed concern about these viewpoints and acknowledged that she would address this by aiming to show similarities as well as differences between Britain and Kenya. She felt the drama session had served as a stimulus which had 'awoken an interest' and had been 'a less dry way of finding out what they know, which is always the first step'.

Mrs J, who is the Humanities Co-ordinator in this large urban school, thought that the drama session was much more effective than more traditional ways of introducing a geography or history topic. Rather than brainstorming or using pictures, Mrs J said, 'When you provide pupils with this type of experience it is bound to get them more interested.'

Mrs T observed that during the drama lesson her class were listening attentively. Although the individuals who spoke most in class were also those who spoke most in the drama, the quieter children were very focused on the drama and were found to be listening, whereas in more traditional teaching situations they would most probably be off task.

Mrs J noted that, as expected, her class responded positively to the drama. Unexpectedly, however, there were a number of children who behaved in a surprising way. Several children who would normally be quiet and reserved took an active role in discussion. Others who would normally be distracted easily were focused and on task throughout. She identified the biggest surprise as Colin losing his self-consciousness and overcoming a serious stammer.

Both teachers commented on the opportunities for developing geographical understanding through drama. They drew up similar lists, which covered such areas as map use, discussion of cultural differences, comparisons with Britain and environmental issues. Other areas highlighted by Mrs T were meaningful opportunities to explore Personal, Social and Health Education issues such as 'doing the right thing, being fair, telling the truth and having respect for others'. Mrs J could see opportunities to examine the historical perspectives of Kenya by placing it on a time line, 'enabling children to understand "this was then" '. The speaking and listening areas mentioned by Mrs T included discussion and debate on stereotypical views, giving advice and persuading others.

Both Mrs T and Mrs J acknowledged the thinking skills required by the pupils throughout the drama session. Mrs J remarked on how the children needed to think beyond the obvious and how this helped them to 'delve into the thinking of others'. Mrs J and her teaching assistant were amazed to observe how the children used their identified 'personal capabilities' naturally when working in drama. These included co-operating with others, behaving appropriately in different situations, sharing ideas with others, listening to other people's ideas and getting involved and showing willingness.

Conclusion

The drama model we have presented was intended to offer an alternative approach, imaginative and arresting, to bridge the gap between what the children know and this 'distant place'. A key product of the creation of a drama context for learning is the promotion of genuine questions and probing from the children, which is not there as spontaneously in other approaches.

When discussing this with the Broad Oak teacher subsequently, she stated that, 'There were lots of opportunities for geography which would have led on. They [the pupils] were stimulated and motivated to learn more. I think this drama lesson could be adapted for a topic on Pakistan.' She suggested using, as the equivalent of the figurine, a hand-carved stand for the Muslim Holy Book, the Koran. As a special object, Mrs J explained that the stand represents the past as most stands today are made of moulded plastic and there is real concern among the Pakistani community that such crafts as wood carving are diminishing in the wake of modern technology.

Finally, although the geography curriculum is identified and linked with objectives and the QCA suggests ways to attain them (QCA 2000), the 'how' is less clearly defined. As we have said earlier, we are not aiming to teach all the geography through drama but to stimulate the interest and enthusiasm of the children which can then be utilised in other sessions.

We had numerous comments at the end of both mornings, for example, 'That was wicked', 'Are you coming again?' 'But you have been working all morning!' Perhaps this is best reflected in the following observation: the Secretary of State for Education said, when introducing the National Primary Strategy (QCA DfES 2003), that children learn better when they are excited and engaged but that what excites and engages them best is imaginitive teaching, because it challenges them and shows them what they can do. He concluded that when there is joy in what they are doing, they learn to love learning. The children in our case study were clearly engaged, challenged, confident and motivated.

References

Beard, C. and Wilson, J. P. (2002) *The Power of Experiential Learning: A Handbook for Trainers and Educators*. London: Kogan Page.

Bradman, T. (1989) *The Sandal*. London: Anderson.

Catling, S. (2003) 'Curriculum contested: primary geography and social justice', *Geography, The Journal of the Geographical Association'*, 88, July.

Cooper, P. and McIntyre, D. (1995) *Effective Teaching and Learning: Teachers' and Students' Perspectives*. Buckingham: Open University Press.

Development Education Centres and membership. Email: devedassoc@gn.apc.org

DfEE (2000) *Developing a Global Dimension in the School Curriculum*. London: DfEE.

DfEE/QCA (1999) *The National Curriculum: Handbook for Primary Teachers*. London: QCA.

DfES (2003) *National Primary Strategy, Excellence and Enjoyment*. London: DfES.

Marshall, D. (1999) *Kenya: World Focus Series*. Oxford: Heinemann.

Moon, J. A. (2004) *A Handbook of Reflective and Experiential Learning: Theory and Practice*. London: RoutledgeFalmer.

QCA (2000) *Geography: A Scheme of Work for Key Stages 1 and 2*. London: QCA.

QCA/DfES (2003) *The National Primary Strategy*. London: QCA.

Weldon, M. (2004) 'The wider world', in Scoffham, S. (ed.) *Primary Geography Handbook*. Sheffield: Geographical Association, pp. 204–15.

SECTION

3

Inclusion and the global dimension

How can we put inclusion into practice in geography?

Justine Slaymaker

Introduction

IN RECENT YEARS mainstream schools have been meeting the challenge posed in the Special Educational Needs Code of Practice (DfES 2001: 7) in respect of 'ensuring all children's needs are met'. The inclusion statement contained within the revised National Curriculum (DfEE/QCA 1999: 30–7) reinforces school responsibility to plan for all learners. It is aimed at supporting the day-to-day work of practitioners and reflects the need for inclusion, an aim embodied in an inclusion statement proposing that:

> Schools have a responsibility to provide a broad and balanced curriculum for all pupils. The National Curriculum is the starting point for planning a school curriculum that meets the specific needs of individuals and groups of pupils.
>
> (DfEE/QCA 1999: 30)

In addition to the National Curriculum inclusion statement there is clarification of how practitioners might meet a diverse range of needs. These are set out in three concise principles:

1 Setting suitable learning challenges

2 Responding to pupils' diverse needs

3 Overcoming potential barriers to learning and assessment for individuals and groups of pupils.

This chapter is both theory- and practice-led. It considers how to embed National Curriculum Inclusion Principles into practice, teaching geography within the primary classroom. Firstly, the relationship between the geography programmes of study and broader inclusive perspectives are explored; secondly, factors, which enable our geography teaching to become more inclusive are outlined and finally two case studies are presented which look at inclusive planning and teaching methods. A series of inclusive lessons at Key Stage 1 are discussed and specific modifications to Key Stage 2 planning in the light of an individual child's Individual Education Plan (IEP) presented.

The relationship between geography and inclusion

Children are encouraged to develop an understanding of their place within the world, through their learning experiences of geography, beginning with developing an understanding of their immediate surroundings. Young geographers are encouraged to investigate their own local community, to ask questions about the people who live and work within it, to develop their understanding of why their community has developed as it has and to explore the positive and possible negative features of their locality. These initial experiences prepare children for the further study of contrasting locations in the extended world. A key aim of the primary geography curriculum is to develop children's understanding of the interrelationship between their home environment and the wider world. Through reaching this understanding children can acknowledge and celebrate diversity both at home and globally and celebrating diversity underpins an inclusive teaching approach. If our aim is to enable children to understand the development of their local community and those that live and work within it we need to ensure that the local school reflects that community. Recognition of the diversity within our schools and their communities is a fundamental step in developing inclusive teaching approaches. This principle was outlined by the 1994 Salamanca declaration:

> The fundamental principle of the inclusive school is that all children should learn together, wherever possible, regardless of any difficulties or differences they might have. Inclusive schools must recognise and respond to the diverse needs of their students, accommodating both different styles and rates of learning and ensuring quality of education for all through appropriate curricula, organisational arrangements, teaching strategies, resource use and partnerships within their communities.

> (UNESCO 1994: 61: 7)

When planning a geography curriculum which maximises participation of all learners, several important factors must be considered. These are outlined in Figure 6.1 and include developing a whole-school ethos, generating positive staff attitudes and ensuring that the National Curriculum Inclusion Principles are embedded in planning. The enabling factors are explored in more depth in the following section.

An inclusive geography curriculum – enabling factors

Developing an inclusive geography can be seen in terms of the factors identified in Figure 6.1.

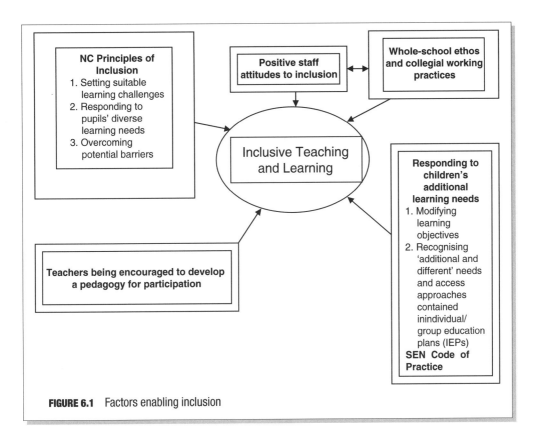

FIGURE 6.1 Factors enabling inclusion

A whole-school ethos

A whole-school ethos with regard to inclusion is essential in order that children have positive experiences of learning geography throughout their school career. Staff need to feel comfortable sharing practices with their colleagues and empowered to seek advice on how to make learning more accessible to children. One element of a whole-school ethos will be reflected in the policy on use of QCA schemes.

Through modifying lesson objectives the geography programmes of study (PoS) can be covered creatively. Modification also ensures that children's prior experiences are taken into consideration when planning, which is essential to ensure inclusive teaching approaches (QCA provide helpful guidance on lesson modification at http://www.standards.dfes.gov.uk/schemes2/geography). For schools not planning geography using the QCA Units' objectives can be simplified by tracking back to the PoS for the proceeding Key Stage or extended by tracking forward. What is of fundamental importance is the avoidance of assumptions about what children can and cannot do. Modification of lesson objectives must not be the result of low teacher expectation of possible attainment but rather as a mechanism to enable children's successful participation and understanding, thus resulting in raised understanding and attainment. As Tilstone, Florian and Rose (1998: 36) assert: 'Teachers who work to develop a curriculum which meets the needs of all pupils are developing a vehicle for inclusion.'

Positive attitudes to inclusion

A step towards avoiding negative attitudes is to celebrate staff expertise and professionalism. Teachers are the experts in identifying the multifaceted approach needed to ensure their class, with its diverse range of learners, can achieve success and enjoyment in learning. Planning geography units of work in partnership with teaching assistants, learning support assistants, teacher and subject leader colleagues is one way of attaining this.

A pedagogy for participation

Inclusive practice involves the ability to recognise the need to apply various teaching styles and approaches. This can be described as a pedagogy for participation. The concept of teaching defined as sociocultural pedagogy by Edwards, Gilroy and Hartley (2002: 107) is useful. This includes notions of:

- teachers as those who assist the interpretations and responses of learners (for example, by modelling, explaining and manipulating the environment);
- pedagogical practice as a process of making judgements about the strategies to be used to assist all learners' increasingly informed interpretations and responses;
- learning environments as sets of opportunities for participation which may provide various degrees of freedom of action.

Starting by looking at the learners within our classrooms and recognising them as the key resource from which relevant and meaningful learning experiences can evolve is at the heart of the National Curriculum principles of inclusion.

Geography has many strong links to other areas of the curriculum. Links with the creative arts can be encouraged. In one inner-city school Key Stage 1 children studying their local area were working on contrasting photomontages of what they liked and disliked about their area using digital camera images.

Barriers to learning can be generated in the way a lesson is planned, the way resources are selected or even by the way in which children are grouped for their activities. Within geography teaching teachers must be particularly sensitive to the materials they select when studying distant places. In *Raising the Attainment of*

Ethnic Minority Pupils (Teacher Training Agency 2000: 34) schools are encouraged to review the curriculum ensuring that materials and resources are selected which:
- recognise and respect the cultural experiences of all pupils
- recognise the contribution to knowledge of a wide diversity of human groups
- promote an understanding of cultural, religious and linguistic diversity
- do not, by omission, ill-informed assumptions or generalisations, reinforce misconceptions about others.

Furthermore, QCA have published guidance with regard to including children newly arrived to the UK (http://www.qca.org.uk). QCA acknowledge that children who have lived overseas are an asset to the geography class due to their first-hand experience of the world beyond the school locality.

An example follows where the Katie Morag story (Hedderwick 1997) was used effectively by school 1 (see Appendix at end of chapter) to develop participation (see Figure 6.2). To ensure her subsequent planning was relevant to the children the class teacher began the first session developing the thought-showers. They were entitled, 'An island is . . .'. The children added their initial ideas of what an island is around a think bubble (see Figure 6.2). The children complete their initial thought-showers in pencil, with the final lesson of the topic allowing the children to add to their thought-shower in coloured pencils. This has a very positive effect on the children, encouraging self-assessment, acknowledging their learning and providing important evidence of individual understanding for the class teacher. Developing thought-showers in this way enables the class teacher to have a clear understanding of what children know and highlights the relevant next step in each child's learning.

The class teacher used a range of classroom organisational approaches. Grouping arrangements were adapted according to the learning objective and activity. The whole class participated in lesson introductions. The introductions were designed to be interactive and peer support was encouraged. The children often used white-boards to scribe ideas. For example, when identifying types of transport found on the island the children were encouraged to note down modes of transport they heard when the class teacher read the Katie Morag story in the lesson introduction. These jottings were used in the main activity when mixed-ability partners identified the type of transport and its purpose. The children with additional learning needs had supportive pictures and 'small world' transport types to sort into categories. When the learning objective involved complex ideas around physical, human features and differences between their own locality and that of the extended world the class teacher used ability groupings in order to revisit the key objective; to know how an island is different from the mainland. Children with additional learning needs created islands using papier mâché. This constructivist approach enabled the abstract idea of an island, which was initially unfamiliar to the children, to become concrete.

Week	Learning intentions	Main activity/classroom organisation	Assessment opportunity/product outcome	Resources	Key vocabulary
3	To begin to understand that the world extends outside their locality (NC PoS 3b). To identify similarities and differences and communicate them (NC PoS 3d).	**Whole-class(W/C) Introduction:** Revisit 'thought-shower' – 'An island is . . .'. Encourage children to add further ideas. Discuss how we live on an island – the British Isles and London – where we live is its capital city. Look at photos of London roads, buildings, etc. Compare to the images of the Island of Coll. In mixed pairs use w/bs to discuss and record differences between the two locations. T to scribe key differences on IWB.	W/C thought-shower responses *An island is...* gp: children's completion of activity sheet	Laminated 'thought-shower' London and Coll photos Whiteboards	Difference Similarity Locality London Isle of Coll
	Revisit key L.I.: to know how an Island is different from the Mainland (NC PoS 3a)	**Table Gps (ability based):** Complete differentiated activity sheets to record at least 2 differences and 1 similarity. Extended to 3 for extension group. LSA gp: begin to make model island. **W/C Plenary:** Build an Island. Chn sit in a circle and select pictures of physical and human features that would be included on the island. Chn discuss with a partner their selected feature. T to check chns understanding of why such features would be included.	LSA: observe chn. constructing papier mâché islands. Prompt using key vocabulary. Ask questions – Where is the land? What surrounds an island?, etc.	Activity sheets Papier mâché	

FIGURE 6.2 Example of inclusive planning in Key Stage 1

When a group of children undertake a different task from their peers it is important that it is valued and recognised as a valid learning experience by their classmates. To achieve this the class teacher forged a link with a secondary Year 8 geography teacher. The primary pupils used their islands to extend a literacy-based project on writing instructions. The instructions were sent to the Year 8 pupils who responded by constructing their own versions and sending photographs of themselves with papier mâché islands. The whole class were very motivated by seeing images of 'big children'. Along with the pictures the secondary pupils devised an island quiz – this allowed the Island Home unit to be explored well beyond the Autumn term.

In addition to a practical approach and a visual teaching style adopted by the class teacher during lesson introductions, a range of multi-sensory resources were developed to support children during the main teaching activity. The resources were carefully used to encourage independent learning.

Many of the class teacher's resources enabled the children to make comparisons with their locality and that of the Island of Coll. Images of London's buildings and transport types were used. For example, the children discussed why Canary Wharf or Sainsbury's would not be found on the Island of Coll. The class teacher felt that examples which were familiar to children would reinforce differences and similarities and prompt quality discussion among the children, which in turn would deepen their understanding.

Speaking and listening using geographical key vocabulary was encouraged throughout lesson introductions and main activities. This supported children's expanding vocabulary in a classroom of speakers of English as an additional language. Children with additional learning needs were also encouraged to use new vocabulary. The class teacher pointed out that visual images were essential for all learners to be able to participate.

Reflecting on this unit of work it is easy to see how the factors which enable inclusive teaching (Figure 6.1) have been met. (It is also worth noting that the class teacher is demonstrating good practice – not a specialist methodology.) The National Curriculum Inclusion Principles are followed through the teacher's visual teaching style, barriers to inclusion are avoided through careful selection of suitable resources and challenging lesson objectives are planned, the use of continuous, ongoing assessment through children's thought-showers assist the class teacher's planning. The class teacher works collaboratively with the learning support assistant assigned to two of her children and the ethos of the class is that all learners are valued. The latter example of practice demonstrates how children with a range of needs can learn alongside their peers.

Responding to children's additional learning needs

Inclusive teaching approaches within the primary geography classroom entail the development of planning to ensure that children with additional learning needs are able to work alongside their peers. The Special Educational Needs (SEN) Code of Practice provides guidance to teachers with regard to meeting the learning needs of children who are described as having learning difficulties. The code defines children with learning difficulties as:

■ having significantly greater difficulty in learning than children of the same age, or

■ having a disability which prevents or hinders them from making use of educational facilities generally provided for children of the same age. (DFES 2001: 6)

The Code makes a very important statement regarding children who speak English as an additional language: these children are not to be regarded as having learning difficulties.

Children with Individual Education Plans (IEPs) should not be regarded as isolated or distinct from the curriculum followed by the rest of the class. Figure 6.3 examines the connection between the whole-class curriculum and IEPs. Wherever possible the National Curriculum Inclusion Principles should be considered to ensure children at School Action and School Action Plus are included in the learning experiences offered to their peers. Indeed, when looking at the inclusion of pupils with additional learning needs Ofsted (2004: 15) found that the most successful lessons were those where teachers incorporated children's personal IEP targets into the learning objectives for the whole class. For example, in one inclusive classroom Year 3 pupils were developing their map skills by drawing a plan of the school for visitors. A pupil described on his IEP as autistic had a personal target to use certain prepositions when speaking. The class teacher emphasised the prepositions during the class introduction and ensured that the child was able to demonstrate their use of the prepositions on a pre-drawn map of the school by instructing their learning support assistant to find certain spaces in the school.

The latter example illustrates 'curriculum overlapping' (DfES 2003). The IEP target of using prepositional language was devised by a Special Needs Co-ordinator, who collaborated with the class teacher and learning support assistant to ensure that much of the child speech and language programme could be incorporated into the child's daily lesson. This avoided withdrawing the child from the classroom and their peers. The current SEN Code of Practice advocates the shared writing of IEPs to ensure the involvement of the class teacher, teaching assistant, learning support assistant, SENCO and the child when devising personal targets. Shared responsibility for the IEPs will ensure that practitioners utilise their understanding of the child

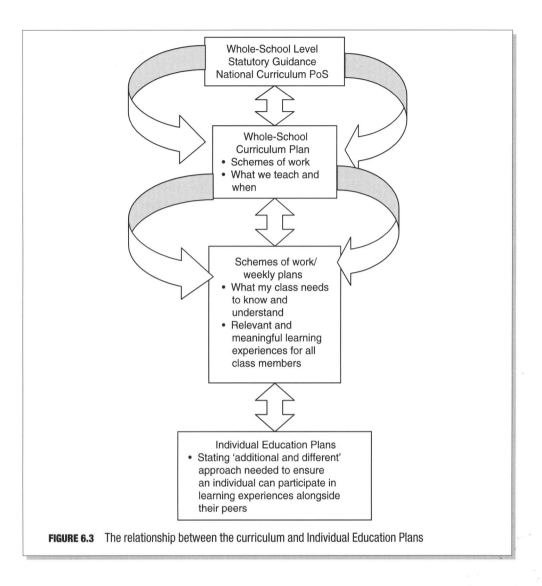

FIGURE 6.3 The relationship between the curriculum and Individual Education Plans

in order that their learning needs are met. This is a positive strategy to enable the inclusion of children with additional learning needs in whole-class experiences. The class teacher's observation and assessment of what his or her class needs to know, understand and do is clearly evidenced through production of teaching plans with clearly specified learning objectives and teaching activities based on meeting all children's needs.

The Code of Practice identifies four main areas of need that may be used to discuss or describe individual pupil's learning difficulties (DfES 2001: 85). They are:

■ communication and interaction;

■ cognition and learning;

- behaviour/emotional and social development;
- sensory or physical.

While background information on children's areas of need is important in order that practitioners can develop suitable, interesting and challenging learning experiences it is important that the areas of need are not used to categorise those children. Labelling children does not enhance inclusive practice and contributes to the notion of a 'deficit model', building an impression of difference and focusing on what a child cannot do. Corbett (1999: 109) states: 'One of the many difficulties associated with labelling individuals within a specific category is that they rarely fit neatly into one slot only but may have many areas of need.'

To ensure children's additional learning needs are met, how should we ensure children participate fully in our geography lessons? The following example uses Unit 20 (DfEE/QCA 2000), 'Local Traffic: an Environmental Issue', with a Year 5 class to effectively respond to children's additional learning needs. Inclusive strategies can prove challenging when children's additional learning needs create a significant gap in ability levels within a class. This example of practice from a Key Stage 2 class illustrates such a challenge and how it was overcome.

In this Unit the Year 5 class considered how the heavily congested A13 road (which runs adjacent to the school) could be improved. The children were encouraged to consider how providing alternatives for drivers might reduce traffic and how this in turn would improve the environment.

To explore this issue the children engaged in geographical enquiry to find out who uses the A13 road, what are the purposes of their journeys, and undertook fieldwork to investigate the impact of congestion within the locality.

The children gathered and recorded their information through the use of surveys and questionnaires. They created leaflets to deter road users from travelling by car and wrote a letter, including their suggestions for improvement, to the local council.

There are 30 children in the class. The class is extremely diverse; 24 children speak English as an additional language. A wide range of languages were spoken by the children in the class, the majority of whom were extremely articulate and able readers and writers who had no difficulty achieving the Unit's outcomes.

The class teacher ensured that she displayed the order of the day's events on a visual timetable. This supported Akbar, a child with complex additional learning needs who finds ad hoc changes to the school day distressing. Akbar uses a picture exchange communication system (PECS) to assist in his learning and recording of work since he often finds communicating orally and in writing difficult. Simplistically, PECS is a system of symbols and text assembled on a Velcro strip which prompts Akbar in speaking, reading and writing. PECS enables him to interact with his peers and his teachers effectively and has lessened his frustration at not being understood. Akbar has a statement of special educational needs which enables him to receive full-time support from a learning support assistant. During planning sessions the learning support assistant was able to suggest appropriate resources to support Akbar in addition to collating appropriate symbols and text for the PECS system.

In order to include Akbar fully in the geography unit of work the class teacher sought advice from the school Special Educational Needs Co-ordinator. The learning objectives were modified to ensure that Akbar could access the initial geographical enquiry. The National Curriculum Key Stage 1 programmes of study informed the modifications to the planning so that Akbar could participate in learning alongside his peers. One of Akbar's interests and areas of strength was in computers and digital media so this was incorporated into the class teacher's planning. During the class's fieldwork Akbar used a digital camera to photograph the congested main road and the surrounding streets to support the classroom-based discussion, leaflet design and letter. To make the issue of congestion and its environmental impact more explicit the Special Educational Needs Co-ordinator suggested that Akbar's focus could be on the danger cars pose, particularly since Akbar's journey to school involved him crossing the A13 and previous personal targets for Akbar had included road safety awareness points.

Following this collaborative meeting several key learning points were established which complemented those being studied by the Year 5 class. These were to communicate by a variety of means (orally, pictorially and in simple sentences) responses to the following geographical questions:

Why is the A13 so busy?

Who is driving all the cars?

Where are they going?

Also, to observe and record:

■ evidence of the congestion on the A13 and the contrasting lack of use of surrounding roads, using digital camera photography;

■ evidence of use of the pedestrian crossings in the locality, again using digital camera photography.

To express Akbar's own views on the safety aspect of crossing the road and whether heavy traffic is clean or dirty, and to make comparisons between digital images which he shared with his peers and printed to send to the local council.

Through modifying the lesson objectives, Akbar was able to create a leaflet deterring car drivers and a PowerPoint presentation of captioned digital images which was shared with his peers and printed off to send to the local council.

Conclusion

This chapter has identified the factors which are essential to acknowledge whether our geography teaching is to be inclusive.

Through their learning of geography, children are encouraged to engage with issues that relate to where they live and to contrasting locations in the UK and the wider world. Through their learning about places they confront diversity and learn about difference. This may involve changing possible stereotypical beliefs about places and the people who live there. Working inclusively makes us as teachers confront issues around diversity, like the children we teach. We learn about diversity and perhaps our own attitudes and beliefs are changed and enriched as a result.

Recognising that inclusion is about ensuring the participation of all learners in their diversity we can see the strengths geography offers as an inclusive subject. Geographical learning does not always have to result in written work. Fieldwork encourages children to use a multi-sensory approach involving observation with all their senses. Enquiry-based learning teaches children that they can ask questions, seek answers and express their views. Investigations carried out both inside and outside the classroom facilitate peer collaboration and supportive class relationships.

When planning and teaching geography the following points were considered by the class teachers featured in this chapter. They serve as a useful checklist for inclusion and include:

- what is the most appropriate way of grouping children in both indoor and outdoor lessons;
- what is the level of adult support offered to children to ensure that independent learning takes place;
- what is the most effective use of available and specifically made multi-sensory resources;
- how personal IEP targets can be transferred into the lesson objectives; and
- how assessment might be used to find out children's previous experiences and the relevant next step required for their future learning.

A thread running through this chapter is that working inclusively involves recognition of the children as the most valuable resource. By finding out what children know as a starting point and creating thought-showers we as teachers can make our geography teaching meaningful. It will assist us in ensuring suitable learning challenges are delivered through effective teaching styles and ensure that barriers to participation are overcome.

Appendix

School 1

The series of practice examples comes from a Tower Hamlets primary school. Situated in London's inner city, it has 540 pupils on roll between the ages of 4 to 11, 85 per cent of whom speak English as an additional language, 75 per cent of whom have free school meals and 15 per cent of whom have special educational needs.

Until July 2005 geography was taught as a distinct subject. The school works from adapted QCA Geography units of work. From September 2005 the school focused upon a themed approach to teaching the curriculum. At the time of this change in focus the teachers were excited about the creative approach to planning offered and the added opportunities to maximise participation of all learners.

In this unit of work the Year 2 children began extending their knowledge and understanding of places through learning about a contrasting locality (see Figure 6.2 for an example of the class teacher's planning).

The Year 2 teacher demonstrates excellent inclusive practice in teaching this Geography Unit. She has 30 pupils in her class, 25 of whom speak English as an additional language, Sylehti being their home language. Five children have complex additional learning needs, three children have a statement of special educational needs which entitles them to 15 hours per week of support from a learning support assistant. Two children are supported at School Action Plus, requiring particular speech and language therapist input.

The learning support asistant contributes to planning meetings and develops multi-sensory resources. The children all have IEPs which indicate their areas of strength, in addition to their areas of need. In this case the children's strengths included their abilities to use drawing as a means of recording. Several of the children in this group were able to add simple text to accompany their visual images.

The 'Island Homes' Unit is covered in the first half of the Autumn term. The Katie Morag stories (Hedderwick 1997) introduced the children to the Island of Struay, based on the real Scottish Island of Coll. The class teacher stressed that this Geography Unit was not a test of children's literacy skills but that one of the Unit's strengths for this particular class was that it was based on a story. The story, coupled with its illustrations, provided a gentle introduction to key geographical vocabulary, some of which would be encountered by the children for the first time in the classroom.

The class teacher employed a visual teaching style when introducing the physical and human features of the Island of Coll. She used web-based resources of real images/photographs to accompany keyword cards. These were held or pointed to as each feature was introduced. The key vocabulary was promoted further in an evolving classroom display. The display board comprised the end-note page in the Katie Morag story, the vocabulary cards and the real images were added as the weeks progressed. The class teacher encouraged the children to take cues from the display when discussing their work both during whole-class and group activities.

The display provided visual support to children during the start of each lesson, where the teacher recapped on children's learning. Whole-class thought-showers were developed and scribed by the class teacher. The class teacher also employed this concept as an individual assessment tool.

References

Ainscow, M. (1999) *Understanding the Development of Inclusive Schools*. London: Falmer Press.

Booth, T. (2003) 'Inclusion and exclusion in the city: concepts and contexts', in Poots, P. (ed.) *Inclusion in the City: Selection, schooling and community*. London: RoutledgeFalmer.

Booth, T. and Ainscow, M. (2002) *The Index for Inclusion*, 2nd edn. Bristol: Centre for Studies in Inclusive Education.

Corbett, J. (1999) *Special Educational Needs in the Twentieth Century: a cultural analysis*. London: Cassell.

DfEE/QCA (1999) *The National Curriculum: Handbook for Primary Teachers in England, Key Stages 1 and 2*. London: HMSO.

DfEE/QCA (2000) *Geography: A scheme of work for key stages 1 and 2* (Update). London: DfEE/QCA.

DfES (2001) *Special Educational Needs: Code of Practice*. London: DfES.

DfES (2003) *Excellence and Enjoyment: A Strategy for Primary Schools*. London: DfES.

DfES (2004) *Learning and Teaching for Children with Special Educational Needs in the Primary Years*. London: DfES.

Edwards, A., Gilroy, D. and Hartley, D. (2002) *Rethinking Teacher Education: Collaborative responses to uncertainty*. London: RoutledgeFalmer.

Hedderwick, M. (1997) *Katie Morag and the Two Grandmothers*. London: Red Fox.

O'Brien, T. (ed.) (2001) *Enabling Inclusion: Blue Skies . . . Dark Clouds?* London: The Stationery Office.

Ofsted (2004) *Special Educational Needs and Disability: Towards Inclusive Schools*. London: HMI.

Teacher Training Agency (TTA) (2000) *Raising the Attainment of Minority Ethnic Pupils*. London: TTA.

Tilstone, C., Florian, L. and Rose, R. (eds) (1998) *Promoting Inclusive Practice*. London: RoutledgeFalmer.

UNESCO (1994) *The Salamanca Statement and Framework for Action on Special Needs Education*. Paris: UNESCO.

Weblinks

The DfES Standards website for geography schemes of work and examples of adapted plans www.standards.dfes.gov.uk/schemes2/geography

The National Curriculum inclusion website at www.nc.uk.net contains useful guidance and assessment criteria for teachers working with children with additional learning needs.

How can children develop an understanding of the global dimension?

Sophie Mackay, Gina Mullarkey and Vimala John

THIS CHAPTER IS written by staff at two Development Education Centres, Cumbria Development Education Centre (CDEC) and one in East London, the Humanities Education Centre, Tower Hamlets (HEC). Both centres support primary and secondary schools in including and developing a global dimension, alongside local community development, in the curriculum.

What is the global dimension?

'The global dimension is concerned with exploring the interconnections between people and places. It asks us to observe the similarities and differences that exist around our world today and relate these to our own lives' (Development Education Association 2004: 2). According to the DfES there are eight central concepts to the global dimension (DfES 2005). These are: Global citizenship; Social justice; Sustainable development; Diversity; Values and perceptions; Interdependence; Conflict resolution; Human rights. Young (2004) gives many reasons why it is important to develop the global dimension of primary geography, for example, interdependence and responsibilities, the need to address discrimination, counter misinformation and stereotypes, the need to live more sustainably and the impact of this on the future. While these reasons will be clear to anyone who has reflected upon the global issues that face us, they may well not be the starting point for developing a global dimension with children.

Different approaches to the global dimension

The eight concepts listed above are designed to provide a conceptual framework for building the global dimension into the curriculum across all subjects. The interpretation of the concepts into strategies for teaching and learning, however, can lead to contrasting approaches. One school of thought begins from the knowledge and understanding of the economic and social forces that shape our lives, with these in turn helping to develop the skills, attitudes and values that empower children. Another interpretation, however, suggests that we should develop the skills, attitudes and values first, as the foundation upon which to build the knowledge and understanding. This chapter attempts to identify a structure around which the global dimension can become a part of the geography curriculum, while avoiding the hazards of teaching approaches which could lead to indoctrination.

Cumbria Development Education Centre has been involved in a number of related projects over the last five years, which take as a starting point the development of a sense of community, and then identifies children's own perceptions of an issue. This is sometimes referred to as a 'baseline'. It is followed by some sort of common input or stimulus. This is broadly the knowledge element, though the stimulus may take the form of a story, a common experience, photographs or artefacts. In all cases the stimulus material is selected for its ability to raise questions. These questions then lead to an exploration of the question or questions selected and finally there is some sort of consolidation of this. The sequence is:

- community building
- 'baseline' perceptions
- a common experience or exposure to an issue
- a group exploration of the issue
- consolidation of the ideas
- some action associated with the issue chosen.

While teachers with an interest in the global dimension will inevitably be keen to see children taking positive action of some sort, it may be years later that the classroom work influences the way that a child responds. Our aim should be to establish thinking and reflective individuals who, in their lifetime, will respond to issues in globally responsible ways. This outcome is far more likely to be realised if we avoid simplistic actions, instead working towards thought out positions. The examples which follow will be linked to the above stages.

Community building

These examples of community builders were used in the joint Cumbria Development Education Centre and Lancashire Global Education Centre School Inclusion and Citizenship Project. This project took place in Barrow's Pupil Referral Unit at Newbridge House in 2005 and at the Brookside Short Stay School in Preston. The activities are largely quick games which enable all members of the community to be perceived, and to perceive themselves, as equal, to build a group identity, and to build group communication skills. The illustrations chosen here all have geographically relevant alternatives which give a place context to the activity.

Globingo

An activity often used to encourage Key Stage 2 children to think about the global dimension is a simple bingo game which highlights the links we all have to places around the world. Each child is given a copy of a sheet of simple questions. (Those in Figure 7.1 were used in the Humanities Education Centre in Tower Hamlets, but there are many other versions available from simple web searches.) They have to complete the grid by moving around the room and asking members of the group the eight questions on the list. The questions are designed to develop thinking about the links they have to other places and to each other. The activity also has a good link to literacy as it requires children to transform a statement into a question. 'Has visited another country' must be changed into 'Have you visited another country?' The grid must be filled in with eight different names and eight different countries. The winner is the first person to complete the grid and call 'globingo'.

Making children aware of the connections they have with the people and places across the world through their everyday lives, the food they eat, the clothes they wear, the toys they play with, is a simple way of introducing the global dimension. It is important that children are made aware of these connections as they are true, real and are a way of connecting what is personal and important to a child with a broader picture of the world, as a system of interconnected people and places.

Beginning with what is personal to the child makes the global connections tangible and meaningful. Asking children to look at and make a list of the places where their clothes were made and then locating these countries on a map or globe is getting them to realise how they are linked to the wider world.

Another example of a community builder, in this case used at Brookside Short Stay School in Preston, follows.

Famous people or places

The group write the names of famous people or places on post-it notes and stick them to the foreheads of their partners, who then have to guess who or where they are by asking the rest of the group questions with yes/no answers about who they are supposed to be. For example, 'Am I in a hot place?', 'Am I in a busy place?' All teachers will have a range of activities like this, but may not always recognise the importance of using them prior to developing any work which aims to develop a global dimension in their curriculum.

The children initially found community building activities very challenging, finding it difficult to take turns, listen to each other, keep hands and feet to themselves, make eye contact, and to take turns in leading, when a lead role existed. These skills,

Find someone who:

1. Has had a visitor from another country to their home.

2. Enjoys eating food from other countries.

3. Has a parent or relative who was born in another country.

4. Has visited another country.

5. Has learned something about another country on TV recently.

6. Enjoys music from another country.

7. Can name a famous sports or film star from another country.

8. Writes to or emails friends or family in another country.

1)	2)	3)	4)
Name _____	Name _____	Name _____	Name _____
Country _____	Country _____	Country _____	Country _____
5)	6)	7)	8)
Name _____	Name _____	Name _____	Name _____
Country _____	Country _____	Country _____	Country _____

FIGURE 7.1 Questions and board for playing globingo

however, are essential for any subsequent serious consideration of the global dimension.

It is also important to include community building activities which enable the community to learn more about each other and therefore feel valued. It becomes particularly important if subsequent discussion takes place using whole-class techniques such as Philosophy for Children (P4C).

Plans were actually altered as the project developed to incorporate a greater number of team-building activities as the benefits of these became more and more apparent.

Community building activities were most successful when the children led them. For example, when visitors from Age Concern joined the group the pupils led some of the community activities, in order to include them in the community.

Children already play games which would be good community builders, therefore remembering to involve students in the process and further developing the community by encouraging movement away from teacher-led learning is quite a natural development. Community builders need to be used every time a new member joins the group, to give them all the chance to get to know each other and regain the feeling of safety they need to participate freely in activities and dialogues.

'Baseline' perceptions

One aspect of the global dimension is the notion of a 'global citizen'. Oxfam's definition (Oxfam 2004) of a global citizen is someone who:

– is aware of the wider world and has a sense of their own role as a world citizen;

– respects and values diversity;

– takes responsibility for their actions.

In the same way that we might begin work on a distant locality through gathering our perceptions of that locality, we might also ask children to define what they think makes a global citizen. By asking children, after a whole-class discussion, to create their own diagram of the types of behaviour that they think global citizenship means we begin to establish some sort of baseline upon which we can build.

Figure 7.2 from work at the Humanities Education Centre in Tower Hamlets, offers one Year 4 child's view of the personal qualities that are needed to be a global citizen, illustrating the relationship between ourselves and the global issues. In this case the child can already demonstrate considerable understanding of the concept of global citizenship. In other cases we have often found significant misunderstandings. In a project to devise 'a survival pack for future citizens' (Cumbria Development Education Centre (CDEC 2004)), children's perceptions of refugees included: 'they are terrorists'; 'aliens'; 'someone not meant to be in England' and 'they never return to their home'.

Sam's Quiz

Tower Hamlets Humanities Education Centre have also designed 'Sam's Quiz' (see list of websites at end of this chapter) as an introduction to the aspects of our lives that have an impact on other places and people around the world. Sam's Quiz is a multiple choice quiz for Key Stage 2 children which appears on the Global

FIGURE 7.2 Year 4 child's view of the personal qualities needed to be a global citizen

Footprints website. The decisions we make each day directly affect us but they can also affect our local community – our schools, our neighbours and the global community. Sam's Quiz focuses on a day in the life of Sam and the personal/local/global impacts of the individual choices she makes throughout the school day. Children's responses to the quiz will provide an idea of their current understanding of global connections and interdependence.

There are seven sections of the quiz: breakfast time, getting to school, in the playground, in the lesson, at work, on the way home, after school. Each section presents a short scenario in which Sam has to decide which decision is the best one to make out of a choice of three. It can be used as a starting point for work on QCA Unit 18 'Connecting ourselves to the world' (QCA 1998) and relates to goal two, 'Learning in a global context', in the DfES international strategy, Putting the World into World-Class Education (DfES 2004).

A common experience or exposure to an issue

Each of the activities below is used as an awareness raiser. In each case questions will be raised from the experiences which can form the basis of subsequent exploration.

Apples

One approach is illustrated by Cumbria Development Education Centre's work in Grizedale forest, where apples which have been imported from different localities around the world are placed at relative distances. On finding the apples the children demonstrate the distance that their apple has travelled by returning to the place where they found the apple or by marking the location on a map of the world.

The key point about these activities is that they need to be kept open as far as possible; they need to include some information and they need to raise questions. Issues such as fair trade, choice, sustainability, interdependence and empowerment cannot be achieved through closed questions or fixed outcomes. Children need to feel involved and they will only feel so if real questions are posed, even if those questions do not necessarily meet the ideal notions of the world held by the teacher.

These shared experiences, and many others, can be found on websites such as 'The Global Dimension', or in publications listed in the References section.

Exploration phase

Philosophy for Children (P4C) is a thinking methodology that encourages the development of questioning and thinking skills, and through dialogue, additionally builds speaking and listening skills. A traditional P4C session starts by the children sitting in a circle and being presented with a stimulus, which can be anything such as a book, a picture, or a visitor. The children, individually or in pairs, then formulate philosophical questions inspired by the stimulus. Their questions are voted on and a dialogue based on the question receiving the most votes then follows. At the end of the enquiry children are asked to make a final statement. The whole process should take a minimum of an hour and this is improved upon as the children become more confident with their skills. Many activities and games can be introduced to the pupils within the traditional session or outside of the session to help develop skills to enable them to gain as much as possible from the process.

P4C aims to help children develop basic skills to boost their self-esteem and intellectual confidence. It aims to create a caring classroom situation where children:

- learn to listen to and respect each other;
- make links between matters of personal concern;
- are encouraged to challenge and explore the beliefs and values of others, and to develop their own views;
- experience quiet moments of thinking and reflection;

- learn to be clear in their thinking and to make responsible and more deliberate judgements;
- learn to be more thoughtful by basing their decisions and actions on reasons.

Prior to using Philosophy for Children the Barrow Pupil Referral Unit project used some specific practical activities to develop skills, before moving into a full enquiry. Here are some examples.

Make a story

The facilitator starts a story (a couple of sentences), then invites someone to swap places and continue the story, then they invite someone else to swap and carry on. Everyone has the opportunity to have a turn. Doing this exercise mixes up the group if they are sitting next to friends, and encourages the development of listening skills as participants assist in developing the story by following on from one another.

I agree; I disagree

The children examine cards depicting behaviour that could be considered as acceptable or unacceptable in their community. They are then asked to go and stand on an 'I agree', or 'I disagree' line. They can stand at either end of the line or place themselves at different points along the line depending on whether they agree/disagree strongly or are undecided. After they have responded to each card the children are asked for reasons for their answers. As a follow up they are asked to come up with other statements of their own which they consider important.

Introducing the term 'philosophy'

A story about Socrates was shared with the children and after reading the story they were encouraged to develop a definition of philosophy. This definition was developed from their learning of who Socrates was and what he did in the story. The group agreed on a shared definition of philosophy as suggested by one student: 'Philosophy lets you listen, think and talk'.

Sorting questions

From a familiar stimulus the students were asked to sort questions into those they knew the answer to, those they could find out the answer to, and philosophical questions, that is questions that have lots of different answers that would be interesting to talk about. The stimulus used with the pupils was the unit of work they had been doing over the previous weeks on the theme of likes and dislikes, so the activity included questions such as, 'Is there litter at Newbridge House?', 'Do we have the power to change the things we don't like?'

Focus on thinking skills

Students revisited some of the skills they think they had developed over the last term. The following activity is adapted from one developed by Ian Patience and Anne De A'Echevarria as presented at the SAPERE (Society to Advance Philosophical Enquiry and Reflection in Education) conference in July 2005. Card bricks with magnets or Blu-tack make up a 'wall', each brick representing a different skill. In pairs, pupils chose a brick from the wall which depicted a skill, for example listening. They then shared with the group how they think they have used and improved the skill they have chosen. Numbers representing their life at different ages were randomly written up by the teacher, 11, 21, 41. There was then an opportunity for everyone to earn extra points if, in pairs, they can explain how they would use this skill now, how they would use it when they are 21 or 41. Each person who comes up with an explanation earns a point for the community. This activity develops meta-cognition; it encourages the children to develop their understanding of different skills and equips them with the ability to question, reflect and challenge.

These activities are short and very focused; this is appropriate for children of different abilities and who have different learning styles.

Consolidation phase

Consolidation involves reflecting and/or acting upon the issue that has been raised in the exploration phase. As stated earlier the 'action' may come many years later and we should be cautious in trying to drive children to actions in the tangible sense. In the case of Cumbria Development Education Centre's work with the Pupil Referral Unit in Barrow-in-Furness (Newbridge House), however, the consolidation did involve adopting a small area of garden in the grounds and developing it, a task that developed from a question raised in the previous discussion, 'Do we have the power to change something that we dislike?' The action was led by the children and resulted from the question.

Local action, 'Global Impact'

Another example is the 2004 Tower Hamlets project called 'Local Action Global Impact'. The focus of the project was improving the local environment. A number of workshops were offered to the participating schools, including working with a whole class or group, to write and illustrate a class story in Big Book format on a theme linked to waste and recycling. The Humanities Education Centre worked with a class to produce a book about looking after the local environment by recycling waste materials. The text of 'The Walk Home' was produced through collaborative story-writing with the whole class. Illustrations for the Big Book were made by collaging waste such as old magazines and newspapers, scraps of cloth. The form echoed the content of the book; a book about recycling made of recycled materials.

Figure 7.3 shows a page from the story. Other examples of children's work from this project and similar projects can be found on the East End Talking website. These illustrate children's consolidation of their understanding of questions related to the global dimension in both local and global contexts.

Consolidation through a literacy task

A persuasive writing activity for Years 5/6 on waste and recycling is based on a newspaper article about the plastic bag ban that is in place in Bangladesh (see Global Footprints website). The writer begins by stating that the ban on polythene bags is to save the city of Dhaka from 'imminent environmental disaster'. What persuasive examples does he use as evidence for this? The following suggested answers were taken from the article.

> '. . . millions of polythene bags disposed of every day . . . clogging Dhaka's drainage system . . .'
> '. . . every day nearly ten million polythene bags are disposed of by Dhaka residents'
> '. . . an overcrowded city which is already suffering from high levels of air pollution and other kinds of environmental hazards'

The writer, although not using any direct quotations, uses different groups to present the arguments: the Government Environment Minister, environmental groups, Dhaka residents. An extract form the resulting leaflet can be found on the website listed 'Dhaka, Plastic'.

Conclusion

Clearly the teaching of geography is concerned with the development of children's sense of place and their knowledge and understanding of the world. Consequently the subject of geography easily lends itself to teaching about the global dimension. This is because, 'thinking geographically involves thinking about you, your place and how your place connects with other people's places' (Geographical Association 'Valuing Places' Statement reproduced in: Lambert *et al.* 2004: 7). It follows from this that the global dimension, enabling children to see how they, themselves and their place are connected to and influenced by global connections, is central to their understanding of place.

Despite searching for one, there are no simplistic definitions for either 'a global citizen' or 'global dimension'. However, references to these terms generally encompass the concept that children should grow up understanding their position, roles and responsibilities in relation to a wider world beyond their own.

The global dimension is central to the development of children's concept of place and their knowledge and understanding of the world. As Simon Catling describes,

'The Walk Home' – teachers' notes

Learning intentions
- To increase children's knowledge and understanding about the value of waste and recycling.
- To explore the potential of reusing materials to create collages.
- To be aware of the negative impact people can have on the local environment.
- To think of ways our local environment can be improved.

Expected outcomes
- Children will have increased awareness about reusing and recycling products.
- Children will produce something for the whole-school community.
- Each child will have a small individual copy of the story to illustrate and keep.

Time	Process/activities	Notes
	Session 1	
	Introduce ourselves – hand out name labels (children can write names while listening to us).	
	Explain aim of the workshop.	Write up some ideas.
	Read *Another Fine Mess* by Tony Bonning (a picture book about the problems caused by people not clearing up after themselves).	List on board.

	Follow with discussion of issues raised.
	  What did that make you think about?
	  What is the message?
	  Ask what things concern them about the world – local/worldwide.
		Separate into those we can/can't do something about.

	Focus on local environment.
	  Tell us some places, streets, landmarks in this area.
	  What do you like/not like about the area?
	  What are some of the things we do that can harm the environment?
		Our group chose:
		Danger to animals caused by litter.
		The unsightly nature of litter in the street.
		The problem of broken glass.

	Focus on the list of those we can do something about. Explain that we are going to write a story which includes some of the things in the list they have just made.	Creating safe places for wildlife to live in.
	Suggest basic story format - Two children walking along. - Who do they meet? - What happens? - How does it end?	
	Teacher scribes main events of story on 10 separate sheets of A2 using children's ideas and suggestions.	Identify children who need support. Move round groups.
	Each group receives a sheet/page with the main events written on. Each child then writes their own version of the events on that page on their own sheet of A4 using the main events page as a prompt.	

Emphasise description, dialogue, vocabulary, and importance of interesting content, must not worry about spelling or handwriting.

Ask children to bring clean rubbish from home – biscuit packets, chocolate wrappers, old magazines/newspapers, material, etc., for use in the collages during the following sessions.

Sessions 2, 3 and 4

Preparation:
Look at every child's writing and edit final story from all contributions. Type up the sections from each child's story to be included in the final version.

Each section of the story should be printed out on a separate page A3/A2.

Write up story: (1) One large print version to fit on A2 pages.
(2) 30 small versions for children.

Create a collage picture to act as a model for what you ask the class to do.

Have example of model collage to help discuss techniques.

In school
Reread story to whole class.

Explain process involved in collage illustration.
Decide together what the characters will look like (continuity).
What size they should be.
Discuss how to include features of the landscape in their picture.

Look at the picture books which have collage illustrations to help generate ideas, e.g. books by Jeanie Baker or Ezra Jack Keats.

Show your model collage to the group.
Emphasise that the image needs to be big and that all the space on the page should be used. Refer to foreground and background.

Give out one A2 sheet per group with the section of the story they were writing in Session 1 on.

Children divide into same groups as previously and start to design the illustration for their page.

One member of the group should write down a list of what needs to appear in the picture to help them remember.

Emphasise the importance of their picture relating to their page of the story.

Tell the group to read through the page of the story that they have decided their picture should include.

Give each group a sheet of coloured sugar paper on which they will create their collage.

Each group uses a pencil to carefully sketch the layout of their picture. Children then select materials from roughly colour-coded boxes of fabrics and paper, cut into desired shapes and stick onto their picture. For those who finish early: ■ Produce front and back covers for the book using collage. ■ Create a key of the different materials used for the collages – describing their texture. ■ Draw a small picture of themselves for acknowledgements page. ■ Start illustrating individual copy. ■ Help with Braille version. ■ Write speech bubbles for characters. ■ Write a blurb for the back cover. Assemble final version Fold big pieces of coloured sugar paper in half and stick the large print version of the written text onto one side and the corresponding collage image onto the other. Repeat for all pages of the story. Decorate the front and back covers. Sew the pages of the book together. Use digital camera to photograph pages. Make A3 colour copy of book/or smaller copies and laminate for more general classroom use.	Emphasise the benefit of choosing a variety of materials with different colours and textures to create an interesting collage.

Resources
Collage materials from Children's Scrap Project, food wrappers, magazines, old fabric and children's contributions, PVA glue, scissors, labels for names, ready-made little books for individual copies, A2 sugar paper, card for front cover.

Evaluation

When listening to the amalgamated version of their stories the class enjoyed recognising how sections of their individual stories had been incorporated into the main story.

The collaging sessions were successful – the class used a good variety of textures and colours when making their images. The contents of the pictures were of a good size and each group made excellent use of the whole page.

At the end of Session 3 we had a good discussion on what the class liked about using collage to create images and how it differed from colouring pencils or paint.

At the end of the final session we had an excellent discussion about the need to protect and look after the local environment. The class were motivated to encourage both their school and their families to do more recycling.

FIGURE 7.3 Example of text from collaborative class book 'The Walk Home'

'the essence of geographical learning is to encourage us all to stop and think about what the world is like, what is happening to it' (Catling 1998: 40).

This chapter has suggested that a key element of teaching the global dimension should be about making time for reflection rather than imposing any predetermined views, opinions or attitudes.

The perception that Global Citizenship must always mean raising in-depth awareness of complex global issues such as poverty, debt, fair trade, human rights, conflict, environmental pollution, is widespread. Without doubt these are all important issues that need to be explored and understood. However the basic 'building blocks' need to be in place in order to do this effectively.

By taking the 'focus' away from specific issues and concentrating on more abstract concepts such as values, attitudes and skills we begin to construct the foundation on which to build knowledge and understanding. For this to be successful, the development of values, attitudes and skills needs to be embedded in sound reflection, emerging from concrete experiences which relate to the children's own lives. It is also fair to say that the projects discussed in this chapter increasingly suggest that it is whole-classroom talk and discussion, facilitated by the teacher asking probing but not closed questions, which promotes the most constructive approaches to global citizenship. In many ways we could see the global dimension developing through the stages of awareness-raising, empowerment and finally commitment (see Cooper 2004). The sequence of learning experiences proposed in this chapter attempts to raise awareness through a common experience and empowerment through group dialogue. Commitment will, we believe, come through a longer-term process of consolidation which we can only begin in the classroom.

Questions for further reflection

Do we make opportunities for talk based on a structured sequence of community building, perception development, shared stimulus, exploration and consolidation?

Do we make pupils aware of the ways in which their lives are inherently linked to those of others around the world?

Do we draw on the diversity within our local community in our teaching about place?

Do the resources we use to teach about place give an all round picture of that place? Do they reinforce or challenge stereotyped ideas that children might have?

References

Carter, R. (1998) *Handbook of Primary Geography*. Sheffield: Geographical Association.

Catling, S. (1998) ' Geography in the National Curriculum and beyond', in Carter, R. (ed.) *Handbook of Primary Geography*. Sheffield: Geographical Association pp. 29-41.

Cooper, G. (2004) 'How outdoor education contributes towards sustainability', *Horizons*, (also available on www.outdoor-learning.org/info-centre/environment.htm).

DfES (1999) *The National Curriculum: Handbook for primary teachers in England – Key Stages 1 and 2*. London: DfES.

DfES (2004) *Putting the World into World-Class Education*. London: DfES.

DfES (2005) *Developing the Global Dimension in the school curriculum*. London: DfES.

DfES/QCA (1998) *Geography – a scheme of work for Key Stages 1 and 2*.

DfES/QCA (2000) *Geography: a scheme of work for Key Stages 1 and 2*. London: QCA. http://www.standards.dfes.uk/schemes2/geography

Jackson, E. (2004) 'Citizenship, PSHE and primary geography', in Scoffham, S. (ed.) *Primary Geography Handbook*. Sheffield: Geographical Association.

Lambert, D., Morgan, A., Swift, D. and Brownlie, A. (2004) *Geography: The Global Dimension. Key Stage 3*. London: Development Education Association.

Oxfam (2004) (first published 1997) *A Curriculum for Global Citizenship*. Oxford: Oxfam.

Qualifications and Curriculum Authority (1998) *Unit 18: Connecting Ourselves to the World*. London: QCA.

Young, M. (2004) 'Geography and the global dimension', in Scoffham, S. (ed.) *Primary Geography Handbook*. Sheffield: Geographical Association.

Young, M. and Commins, E. (2002) *Global Citizenship – The Handbook for Primary Teachers*. Oxford: Oxfam.

Weblinks

CDEC (Cumbria Development Education Centre) resources named below can be purchased by contacting cdec@ucsm.ac.uk or visiting http://www.cdec.org.uk

CDEC (2003) A Survival Pack for future citizens

CDEC (2004) Exploring Values

CDEC (2006) Energy Island, A School Linking Project (2005)

CDEC (2005) Philosophy for Global Citizenship Project (using P4GC to support learning in global citizenship)

Outdoor Learning 2005 www.outdoor-learniong.org/infocentre/environment.htm

CDEC School Inclusion and Citizenship Project. An article about this is available at http://sapere.org.uk/files/SchIncProject.doc The full report is on the NWGEN (North West Global Education Network) website at http://www.globdimnw.fireflyinternet.co.uk/

Humanities Education Centre (Tower Hamlets) material refers to the following websites

East End Talking www.eastendtalking.org.uk

GlobalFootprints www.globalfootprints.org

Sam's Quiz http://www.globalfootprints.org/active/Dayinthelife/quiz1.htm

PersuasiveWriting/Dhaka plastic http://www.globalfootprints.org/pdf/waste_lit56.pdf
DfID education website The Global Dimension www.globaldimension.org

The Geographical Association www.geography.org.uk/global

SAPERE The Society to Advance Philosophical Enquiry and Reflection in Education
http://www.sapere.org.uk
London and the South East region Global Dimension teachers' website Local 4
Global www.local4global.org.uk

The North West Global Education Network www.globaldimensionnw.org.uk

Values, enquiries and cross-curricular approaches

Is geography suitable for the Foundation Stage?

Jan Ashbridge

'WHAT'S THE POINT of teaching geography to Foundation Stage children? They don't even know where here is!' This is an opinion that I have heard from Foundation Stage practitioners, geography co-ordinators in primary schools, and, in more measured words from lecturers at college. Geography seems to be something that begins in Key Stage 1 and has not had the highest priority in the early years in the eyes of many. When the Curriculum Guidance for the Foundation Stage (CGFS) (DfEE/QCA 2000) was introduced, it must, at first sight, have seemed that geography had vanished from the curriculum for 3- to 5-year-olds. In fact the word geography occurs only once in the document (on page 82). Since its introduction, the culture of teaching discrete subjects has changed to a less compartmentalised curriculum for our youngest children and the 'G word' seems to have fallen out of use, to be replaced with the less scientific, less specific word, 'place'. Is it a case of out of sight, out of mind?

Joy Palmer, in *Geography in the Early Years* (1994: 3), says that geography with young children is 'fundamentally about the development of the concepts of space and place'. Space and place are words that crop up frequently in the Curriculum Guidance for the Foundation Stage and not just in Knowledge and Understanding of the World, but across all areas of learning. Could it be that rather than being dead, geography has simply been 'missing in action', waiting to be rediscovered?

With the status of geography unclear in the eyes of many involved in Foundation Stage education, it is important to explore the value of geography to young children, the skills and concepts that children bring with them and how these can best be developed in Foundation Stage settings (Cooper 2004).

What do children already know?

Children are skilled observers of the world around them and as co-constructors of knowledge and skills they have been interacting with and exploring their environment and information gathered from important adults in their lives. By the time they enter our settings their ideas and concepts will have been formed through this two-way dialogue and exchange.

Children come to our schools and other settings with a wide range of knowledge and understanding, and will already have a complex and sophisticated set of geographical skills and concepts that they are trying out and honing. What makes it complicated for practitioners is that, as Joy Palmer (1994) observes, each child has their own 'world inside their heads'; they have their own unique outlook on the world, their own individual understanding and interpretation of what they experience and observe. We must try to get an idea of how the child views the world they live in if we are to take forward their geographical understanding and make geography meaningful for them.

So, it is vital that we spend time finding out what sense children have made out of what they have seen and experienced because their conclusions may be very different from our own. Again, Palmer usefully points out that, as an individual, each child:

> has a unique relationship with the world in which he or she is growing up: a relationship based on feelings, experiences, and interactions with people, places, objects and events.
>
> (Palmer 1994: 2)

Our role is a tricky one. We must discover and value the child's views and understanding while at the same time identify flaws and misconceptions in their knowledge. Children do not have the same amount of direct contact with their environment, near or far, as we adults do. Much of the information they get from the world around them is filtered through us as adults. We often choose what books they should read and what television they see. The adult world decides what images go on posters and what information children get at school. Adults also give children their own opinions and value judgements by the way they talk to children about different peoples and places. Most of our young children's information on the wider world comes through these secondary sources, but despite this they are adept at making their own observations of this limited worldview. They are always trying to link these limited perceptions with the immediate environment they see around them. With this information they make and test hypotheses on which to base the 'world inside their head'. This can understandably lead to confusion and errors in their understanding.

What should the curriculum look like?

The Geographical Association (2003), in its own strategy for the Foundation Stage, recognises that children's existing knowledge needs to be affirmed and encouraged in order to give them the motivation and confidence to take their learning forward. Drawing on their existing knowledge engages their curiosity and this supports us, the practitioners, in challenging and extending their understanding, while at the same time sensitively challenging and balancing misconceptions and misinformation.

Blyth and Krause (1995) put forward a curriculum model for geography that contains four main strands:

- the local area
- nearby places
- distant places
- the wider world.

This is important for Foundation Stage practitioners to be aware of, as Blyth and Krause argue that all of these strands should be represented at all stages of development. This clearly challenges the more accepted approach that Foundation Stage children should be encouraged to develop their knowledge and understanding only of their local area. In the Early Learning Goals for a Sense of Place, the Curriculum Guidance for the Foundation Stage talks in terms of children being able to 'observe, find out about and identify features in the place they live and the natural world' and to 'find out about their environment and talk about those features they like and dislike' (DfEE/QCA 2000: 96). Far from the wider world suggested by Blyth and Krause, the CGFS suggests that geographical skills are developed but used in the narrow context of the local area.

Starting from the child and their own place in the world is a logical viewpoint, which has been researched and expounded for many years. It is common sense, as well as based on the principle of first-hand, active learning situations. However, this can in effect limit and restrict our young children's view of the world and thereby inhibit their ability to adequately make sense of their world. It would seem that perhaps simply helping them to explore and make sense of their immediate environment might not be enough. Should we also be supporting their ever-increasing awareness of places and people beyond their own immediate environment?

The Chief Inspector of Schools, points out in his Annual Report (Bell 2005: 6) that unless the practitioner is 'geographically aware' then children's own limited experiences of the world restrict the potential of further geographical discovery through play. Part of the problem is that we, as practitioners, often have little up-to-date, unbiased information and understanding about different cultures and different parts of the world. We shy away from teaching that which we feel we do not fully understand ourselves rather than face questions that we cannot answer. It is often easier for us, the adults, to support children's developing knowledge of the local environment as we know it well ourselves, but would find it difficult to help children understand the life of, for example, native American peoples without drawing on stereotypical images and information from our own childhoods.

Children's sense of place does indeed begin with the immediate space they are in. They need to have access to the outdoor environment in order to establish their place in it and to explore different kinds of place: the muddy place where the water doesn't drain away, the sloping place where the ball will roll away, the hard place where the ball will bounce, the shady place under the tree and so on. Children are fascinated by their environment and enjoy exploring it. They come to school with a wide range of geographical vocabulary and a pressing desire to use it and put it in context. They also have a need to scout the area and know each nook and cranny. Risk taking, both in behaviour and in learning, is more in evidence when the children are able to develop their skills outdoors. Children are able to build upon first-hand experience, which provides a lot of prior knowledge, and most are motivated to participate. It is important to take advantage of natural curiosity in a situation where children are asking questions, solving problems and observing and recording outcomes in quite spontaneous ways. Young children learn best through play and the Curriculum Guidance for the Foundation Stage recognises that play, both outdoors and indoors, is the key way in which children learn, and that it is:

> Through play, in a secure environment with effective adult support, [that] children can explore, develop and represent learning experiences that help them make sense of the world.

> (DfEE/QCA 2000: 25)

It is our role as adults to provide both planned and structured play activities focused on geographical skills and understanding, and opportunities for children to learn through their own child-initiated play activities. The latter involves practitioners planning and structuring, not the activities themselves, but the resources and the environment in which the play occurs. The examples that follow describe activities that are adult initiated, child initiated and there are some where this distinction is blurred and the adult and child are learning together, co-constructing knowledge and understanding through conversations, exploring real and imagined environments together and using resources such as photographs and video to reach a common understanding. At the heart of all the examples described in the following pages is a commitment to the principle that play and playful activities are at the heart of the geographical experiences and opportunities offered to the children.

The world outside the window

Play involving children imagining and creating their own worlds is very common during outdoor play, and a little forethought on the part of the practitioner can support the development of new geographical understanding and skills in many ways. For example, a favourite theme with Foundation Stage children is camping.

Alongside tents, backpacks and compasses, I have given laminated maps of the local area to children. Access to such maps gives opportunities to find familiar places, become familiar with how maps look and trace rivers and roads.

I have observed that many children are able to interpret some of the symbols, such as that for a church, from their own knowledge of churches. This rapidly leads to them drawing their own maps as they go off on their travels, either to find their own way or to leave for friends coming later. Sensitive adult involvement and observation of this play enables one to assess the understanding that the children have and plan further input through either information or resources in order to extend their knowledge and to support children in applying this new knowledge in appropriate ways. Children are often able to draw maps even before they can read or write and can use maps they have drawn to retell a journey or a storyline from their play. In my outdoor area, children often used sticks, stones or chalks to leave trails for each other to follow, using arrow shapes to point the way. After observing this play, it was decided to support the children by providing them with a treasure chest, complete with beads and bangles. One storyline that developed involved a giant stealing treasure. A group of children created a trail to follow that would lead to the giant's hideout and the recovery of the chest. Accompanied by an adult, for moral support because the giant was really rather frightening, a group of children set off to follow the trail. The playground and its surroundings faded away, to be replaced by dark tunnels, long, winding paths and steep hills. The children were able to use and show their understanding of a wide range of vocabulary to describe their imaginary landscape and the adult was able to supplement and support this where appropriate. Children were able to communicate their geographical experience in a range of ways and recorded the route using different and individual methods and resources. Some drew maps; some wanted to take photos to make into a book to tell their story; Holly used play dough to make a more 3D representation of the journey she had made.

The ability to communicate their knowledge and understanding after the event helped them to remember it and describe it to others long after the play itself. Indeed the book became a firm favourite in the book corner. These kinds of activities, given time and space to develop outdoors, as well as adult encouragement and support, are very important in developing geographical skills in Foundation Stage children. Skills, on their own, are not enough. Children need to develop attitudes and values to support their appreciation of the world around them.

Using the outdoor environment is also a key way to help children become interested in and aware of the beauty of the natural and built up environments around them. It is likely that their attitudes towards the environment are already being shaped for good or ill by their parents and other important adults. Practitioners have a vital role to play in fostering a sense of responsibility for the environment and the plants and animals that share it with us. To do this, a box of equipment for children to use and explore could be made available for children whenever they are working outdoors. Children need access to binoculars, for watching birds and seeing far away; magnifying bug boxes, for close up examination of minibeasts and other small items; pond dipping nets; and magnifying glasses, as well as appropriate books and labelled pictures for identifying things that they find. An interested, enthusiastic and informed adult is also essential! Experiences such as these are vital in helping children to develop their own budding enquiry skills. Their questions become less general as their individual interests take them into more specific areas of activity.

Children ask and try to answer fundamental geographical questions every time they engage with the outdoor learning environment. Seven key questions have been identified as fundamental to children's learning in geography (Foley and Janikoun 1996:1):

- Where is this place?
- What is this place like?
- Why is this place as it is?
- How is this place connected to other places?
- How is this place changing?
- What is it like to be in this place?
- How is this place similar to, or different from another place?

These questions help practitioners to focus on geographical enquiry skills with the children whether during planned or child-initiated activities. When children are engaged in learning in a well-planned outdoor environment, they are likely to be, at various points, fully involved in grappling with these seven questions. This happens through the geographical skills of observing, investigating, gathering information and discussing with other children and adults. It can be seen that young children 'invest their surroundings with personal meaning and interpret it according to their needs' (Scoffham 2004: 18). They invest their environment with meaning far beyond the literal and actual, as can be seen in the example discussed earlier and the children's imaginative response to the treasure chest. Each child could have a different answer to questions such as the second one above, 'What is this place like?', as each would have an individual emotional response to the environment they are in.

Encountering the changes in the outdoor environment gives children first-hand experience with which to start considering the question 'How is this place changing?' They can observe the seasons rolling round, birds arriving, trees budding, frost forming and sun drying up puddles, etc. As Helen Bilton succinctly puts it, 'children need to have experience of these weather features – not be stuck inside looking at it!' (Bilton 2002: 62).

The world beyond the playground

Moving from the knowledge of the here and now to that of more distant places can seem quite a challenge to some practitioners and children. It is very useful to be able to draw on children's actual knowledge of other places they have been to and also the deeply real (in a different sense) world of their imaginations. A 'magic carpet' can provide children with a way of exploring places and environments further and further removed from their own. Letting children decide where the carpet should travel to is a good way of finding out what sort of places they know about. For example, children often choose to go initially to places they themselves have visited, such as the beach, the zoo, the shops, or to places someone they know has visited. Finding out what these places are like for the children requires them to use many of the same skills they would use to explore their real surroundings but relies also on their ability to remember features they observed and emotions they experienced while there, often coupled with a liberal dash of imagination. Giving children familiar props such as binoculars, magnifying glasses, notebooks and clipboards to record their visit, encourages them to use established geographical skills in a creative way. This hopefully helps to enlarge and add detail to the 'world inside their heads'. A book that has been successfully used to extend this idea further is *The Earth from the Air for Children* (Arthus-Bertrand 2002). The beautiful photographs of different places around the world were used as the stimulus for magic carpet rides to visit them. The places were found on a map and plans were drawn up for the trip. Can they tell what the weather will be like? What sort of clothes will they need to take? Are there any people there? Once there, the children are again able to use their skills and developing knowledge to explore their new environment. Adults can support by pointing out items of interest, a colourful bird, a market stall, a particularly interesting tree and so on, depending on the destination. Children can begin to appreciate what it might really be like to be there and how this new environment is similar to their own.

All the way to China

Young children, however, are able to form a deeper understanding of their own surroundings by the act of comparing them to places which are in some way very different from their own. Some children will have actual experiences of different places to draw on because of their backgrounds and family life but, for some, these opportunities need to be provided for them in the setting. This of course can come about through planned activities, such as those described above, but also through making the most of opportunities that present themselves to us.

While I was working with a Reception class, we almost fell into a project on China. It was nearing Chinese New Year so some work was planned to help the children find out about the country but one of the families represented in the class was in the final stages of adopting a baby from China. This meant that the country was being named often in a variety of contexts. It soon became apparent that the children had many ideas and concepts about China and its people. The majority had celebrated Chinese New Year in the Nursery class the previous year, but as the school was in a predominantly white area they did not have a great deal of first-hand knowledge about the Chinese culture or people. So, where had these ideas and concepts come from? Were they accurate? The following excerpt from a conversation took us by surprise:

Mrs A: I wonder what it's like in China.
Steven: If you see a cave that means you're there. I think they are born in the olden days.
Mrs A: Why do you think that?
Steven: Because dragons live in China and because dragons are in the olden days.

This was a salutary lesson to us about the power of a good story well told. It has long been recognised that story is an excellent way to introduce children to different places, stimulating their curiosity and imagination. In this case, the story they had been told in Nursery about the origins of the Chinese New Year; and the monster, Niang, who lived in a cave in the mountains, had engaged the children at such an emotional level that this was real for them. They had also made a dragon with boxes and fabric and had danced with it. Steven believed that this was what modern-day China was like. He had never had any experience of China or of dragons except through the story and the dance, so if China was real then why not dragons? The children had a picture in their heads about what the China of this story was like, hence the references to a place from long ago. The issue came up again when we talked with the children about planning the role-play area, which was to be a Chinese home. Some children tried to think about what it might be like:

Christopher: They've got sticks for their houses.
Chloe: What? Sticks in the house?
Christopher: No – in the ground.
Chloe: Why?
Christopher: Sticks for the side and for the top, and like straw on the top like in the pigs' story.
Mrs A: A thatched roof? How do you know that Christopher?
Christopher: I've seen it in a picture.

Christopher already had some knowledge of houses from the past and knew from books that at some time houses had been made out of timber and thatch and felt that if China was long ago then this is what the houses must be like. For Christopher, time and place were getting confused. Perhaps I should not have been so surprised. Time and place are both concepts that it is hard to experience directly and require a lot of imagination and empathy to develop. Children, in their play, spend large amounts of time re-creating different imaginary places and times, and as they grow older and more experienced they can combine their creativity with greater knowledge and understanding. By having a curriculum in the Foundation Stage that does not compartmentalise children's learning, practitioners are more able to flexibly develop understanding in a more holistic way.

During an early discussion the children were asked where they thought China was. This question threw up some interesting ideas, which showed the children trying to use information and vocabulary that they had already acquired from either personal experience or secondary sources of information:

Alison: I think it's very far away.
Gareth: Near New Zealand on the east side of the sea.
Alison: It's a very hot place.
Children: Yeah!
Mrs A: Why do you think it's hot there?
Alison: Because it's very far away. You'd go on your holiday, so it's hot.
Sarah: Might be near Disneyland. I went on my holiday there.
Elspeth: I think there's a desert in China because hot places are where there is a desert, OK?

The children were using geographical vocabulary such as east, sea and desert in sensible and convincing ways. They had the idea that it was not anywhere near where they were currently and made a link between far-away places and holidays which recalled what they already knew. The school has several links with New Zealand through different families emigrating and visiting for holidays and we had previously discussed how far away, it was. Therefore, if China was far away, it must be near New Zealand. It's usually hot on your holiday so it makes sense to them to assume that China is also hot. Elspeth uses more geographical knowledge; she is aware that deserts are very hot places and links this information to her concept of this far-away place.

Children did have some information from their own first-hand experience. The local Chinese take-away was run by a Chinese family and they had nearly all had some Chinese food either from there or at the Nursery Chinese New Year Celebration and had tried to eat it with chopsticks. They knew some of the food that people in China might eat and that they used chopsticks instead of knives and forks. This factual information seemed more useful to us adults as it gave us something concrete to plan from. Perhaps we could build on this knowledge to help the children develop a more realistic image of modern-day China. Their initial ideas about clothing showed they were influenced not by what they had seen the Chinese family wear in town but by images from books, for example *Celebrations* (Kindersley and Kindersley 1997).

Ben:	Chinese people wear black dresses and red dresses. I've seen it in a book.
Mrs A:	Do you think everyone wears them?
Ben:	No . . . yes. They've got trousers too. Shiny.
Elspeth:	YES! I've got some at home. They were a present. Like shiny pyjamas. I'll bring them to show.

We learned from conversations with the children that although they knew that the Chinese family in town did not wear clothes like these, in 'the world inside their heads' Chinese people wore the stereotypical tunics and pyjama-style outfits. Where had they found this information? Once again the story of dragons and caves may have been to blame but also images that they had been shown in children's information books about Chinese New Year when all the children are dressed up in more traditional clothing. Perhaps it had never been explained to the children that children didn't always dress like this, or it might have been explained, but what stuck in the children's 'world inside their heads' was the captivating pictures it conjured up. Children also had dressing-up clothes at home and in school that reflected this image and perpetuated the misconception.

So, through the pictures, stories and resources that had already been shared with the children, adults seemed to be adding to the misconceptions and stereotypical ideas, rather than taking children's learning forward, changing attitudes and creating new learning. Something needed to be done before we celebrated Chinese New Year again and the opportunity presented by the adopting family seemed an ideal one to broaden the children's awareness of China beyond the festival and into the everyday life and culture of the people.

We started from the understandings and concepts that the children already had and their enthusiasm for the story they remembered so well. They felt confident and comfortable with the story and enjoyed talking, playing and exploring it in a variety of ways. Through asking open-ended questions, we were able to encourage children to think a little beyond the original story and start to think about their 'knowledge' and question it:

James:	The old man . . . [in the story] he came on a donkey. Cars aren't invented in China yet.
Mrs A:	OK, how do you think Francis' mummy and daddy will get to China when they go to collect his new sister?
Francis:	They are going on an aeroplane.
Mrs A:	Aeroplanes are invented in China then?
James:	Yes, you can't go to China in a car, it's over the sea.
Francis:	You can't put a baby on a donkey, it'll fall off.
James:	Maybe if they've got aeroplanes, they have cars too? They do in New Zealand.

Here, adult and children are both involved in constructing knowledge. The adult is supporting the children's developing knowledge through being involved in the children's own point of interest. The interaction starts from the child's current understanding and, through questions and supporting discussion, the understanding is developed and changed. Siraj-Blatchford describes these kinds of interaction as 'sustained shared thinking interactions' (Siraj-Blatchford *et al.* 2002). During these kinds of adult–child interactions the practitioner is looking to scaffold and support children's learning while at the same time allowing them time to explore concepts and think for themselves. Questions are used not just to assess what the child knows but also to help them speculate and extend their understanding.

To encourage this further, the children were presented with a range of photographs of modern-day China on the interactive whiteboard and were supported in looking for similarities to things they knew from their own life. The interactive whiteboard was a very useful tool. Using it motivated the children enormously, especially when they were able to watch video footage on the big screen of people going about their everyday business in different parts of China as well as taking part in New Year celebrations. Adults used open-ended questions to encourage the children to make their own connections between what they were seeing and their own life and environment. A large-scale map of the world on the interactive whiteboard and information from the family who were adopting the Chinese child enabled us to see how far away the country was and how you could get there. A carefully resourced and organised role-play area set out as a Chinese home gave children the opportunity to talk about their new and emerging knowledge and understanding and, importantly, put it into a meaningful and relevant context.

By the time the theme had come to an end, children had a more realistic perspective of what it might be like to live in China. They had a heightened appreciation of the diversity of peoples and places in the world. They could talk about where in the world China was, using other countries such as Japan as pointers and they knew that you would need to get there on an aeroplane. One child was going on holiday to Australia and was able to show on a map where the two countries were in relation to one another. Children knew that while special clothes were sometimes worn, children in China often dressed just as they did, and played similar games with balls and dolls. Photographs of city life in China and contrasting rural images were discussed, as were similarities and differences. Being from a rural community with children from several farming families in the class, the children were able to connect their own experiences with those of the children in the photographs. They particularly enjoyed looking at the photographs of children in school:

Mark: The school looks a bit like ours but it's made of bricks not stone.
Richard: Does it have the same stuff in?

Mark: Well . . . look. [Look at the photo together] There, that's a computer.

Allan: They've got a whiteboard like ours for writing on . . . and . . . and a little telly.

Richard: We don't have a telly every day; we only have it some days. Maybe theirs isn't there all the time?

Mark: They have singing too. See they've got a CD player.

Allan: Can you see their toys? Have they got sand and stuff?

Mark   Can't see. It's just the front of the classroom. Maybe they are at the back.

Rachel: I think they go in normal clothes . . . see, and we have to go in school uniform. Not really that different is it though?

Through listening to and observing the children's thoughts and understandings about this far-away place, we were able to provide appropriate resources and teaching input to help the children move from a purely imagined, fictional China, to a real place where children go to school and sing and write on whiteboards while wearing normal clothes. I still don't think they quite believed me about the dragon though.

So why should we teach geography to young children?

The natural curiosity and spirit of enquiry that is evident in young children make it a perfect time to develop their skills and understanding. They will ask questions; they will use any available source to try to create their own ideas of what places and people are like. If we, the practitioners, do not support these skills by presenting them with realistic, unbiased, unstereotypical images of different cultures, places and people, then all they have to go on is their own limited world view and the, sadly, often biased, view fed to them by the adult world. Young children will see links, they will try to understand China, like Christopher and Steven did, but without the right information and sensitive adult involvement they'll get it wrong and will perpetuate misunderstandings.

Alongside the need to counteract their misconceptions, children deserve to have access to correct information and images of the world both near and far. Joy Palmer argues that no child is too young to begin to stand in awe of the world, to reflect on the glories of the natural environment and the achievements of human life, or to take those first steps along the path towards individual concern, responsibility and action (Palmer 1994: 180). This is true, whether the awe the child feels is found in the realisation that school children in China have a television and a whiteboard, or is found in the birds and trees and even architecture that fringe their own playground. In either case we equip children to face the world with an attitude of individual concern, responsibility and action.

References

Arthus-Bertrand, Y. (2002) *The Earth from the Air for Children*. London: Thames and Hudson.

Bell, D. (2005) *'Geography in Primary schools': The Annual Report of Her Majesty's Chief Inspector of Schools 2004/5*, 20 October. London: HMSO. http://www.ofsted.gov.uk/publications (accessed 23 October 2005)

Bilton, H. (2002) *Outdoor Play in the Early Years*, 2nd edn. London: David Fulton Publishers.

Blyth, A. and Krause, J. (1995) *Primary Geography: A Developmental Approach*. London: Hodder & Stoughton.

Cooper, H. (2004) 'Why time? Why place? Why play', in Cooper, H. *Exploring Time and Place Through Play*. London: David Fulton Publishers, pp. 5–23.

DfEE/QCA (2000) *Curriculum Guidance for the Foundation Stage*. London: DFEE/QCA.

Foley, M. and Janikoun, J. (1996) *The Really Practical Guide to Primary Geography*. Cheltenham: Stanley Thornes.

Geographical Association (2003) *Making Connections: Geography in the Foundation Stage – a position statement from the Geographical Association*. Sheffield: Geographical Association.

Kindersley, B. and Kindersley, A. (1997) *Celebrations*. London: Dorling Kindersley.

Martin, F. and Owens, P. (2004) 'Young children making sense of their place in the world', in Scoffham, S. *Primary Geography Handbook*. Sheffield: Geographical Association, pp. 63–91.

Milner, A. (1994) *Geography Starts Here*. Sheffied: Geographical Association.

Palmer, J. (1994) *Geography in the Early Years*. London: Routledge.

Scoffham, S. (2004) 'Young geographers', in Scoffham, S. *Primary Geography Handbook*. Sheffield: Geographical Association, pp. 15–23.

Siraj-Blatchford, I., Sylva, K., Muttock, S., Gilden, R. and Bell, D. (2002) *Researching Effective Pedagogy in the Early Years. Research Report No. 356*. London: DfES.

How can geography make a significant contribution to a coherent and meaningful Key Stage 1 curriculum?

Kevin Hamel and Katharine Langley-Hamel

Transition from Foundation Stage to Key Stage 1

A CENTRAL ASPECT of the Foundation Stage curriculum is the development of skills, knowledge and understanding to help young children make sense of their world and 'to find out more about the world they live in and the people they encounter' (DfEE/QCA 2000a: 82). The *Primary Geography Handbook* observes that, 'Geography is at the very heart of early learning, encompassing as it does aspects of social, physical and cultural worlds that are necessary for meaningful understanding of our surroundings' (Martin and Owens 2004: 63).

This chapter investigates ways in which Key Stage 1 children can build on the secure foundations established within the area of learning, 'Knowledge and Understanding of the World'. Opportunities for children to explore their environment are reflected in the early learning goals in this area for 'A Sense of Place' (DfEE/QCA 2000a). This aspect, focusing on children's observations about the natural world and the environment in which they live, develops the skills and understanding to promote a successful transition to the Key Stage 1 geography curriculum. Critically, the chapter shows how a geographical focus may lead to imaginative and creative work involving musical mapping, literacy and ICT. 'Children's early experiences of place may vary enormously but they all bring some awareness and understanding of geographical concepts to early learning contexts' (Martin and Owens 2004: 63).

Story as an integral part of Key Stage 1 geography

Story seemed to be an appropriate starting point to help children develop their understanding of a sense of place. The power of story in children's learning has been well documented; Wells (1987) established clear links between children's early experience of listening to stories and subsequent success in school. He noted the importance of story in helping children to decontextulise and develop skills in abstract thought. Goodwin and Perkins (1998) note the importance of story in children's linguistic, personal and conceptual development. Through narrative, young children make sense of their experiences and of the world in which they live and develop the vocabulary they need to express this understanding.

Lewis (2004: 150) notes the important contribution of geography to children's language and literacy development. 'When studying geography, we need not only to use technical and scientific language to explain places, features and processes, but also to employ descriptive, aesthetic and emotive language in expressing personal responses to places or issues.'

Building on children's early experiences of story and sense of place, this chapter explores ways in which a shared story can present a framework for developing children's skills of geographical enquiry through description, and understanding of, their local area, and comparison with other places. It was also felt that a shared story was an excellent vehicle for making meaningful links across the Key Stage 1 curriculum.

Creativity and context

In order to explore the creative links between story and geography, a small project was set up in two very different Key Stage 1 classrooms. The aim was to consider the ways in which story could be used to support the Units 1 and 3 (DfEE/QCA 2000b). Detailed consideration was given to the creation of meaningful cross-curricular links between geography, literacy and music. The schools were selected for their contrasting localities; the former was in a remote rural location on the Cumbrian fells, the latter in a richly diverse area of inner-city Manchester. A story was chosen which, (we hoped) related to the children's lives. This focused on a birthday, a trip to the shops to buy food and a surprise present. Frequent breaks in the story invited children to respond and fill in the gaps drawing on their own experiences and to visualise the journey from their homes to the shops, recalling key features seen and heard. The children's contributions were scribed to ensure that the need to write did not inhibit their responses. Through their contributions to the story, the children were able to address learning objectives from Unit 1. Through their collaborative responses, the children explored their sense of place in relation to home and school. Subsequently, both schools decided that they wished to develop their association and planned to exchange digital photographs of the school surroundings and begin an email correspondence between children in the two classrooms.

The power of story

It was thought that encouraging children to collaborate in storytelling would help children to develop the skills, knowledge and understanding outlined in the QCA long Unit 1, Around Our School – the local area. Specifically the activities addressed the learning objective. What are our immediate surroundings like? Activities resulting from the story provided opportunities for children to take part in an enquiry, to follow a route, to make maps and plan and to use relevant geographical vocabulary. The subsequent involvement of a storyteller from Africa, who adapted the basic story framework to a different context, extended the learning opportunities and addressed several aspects of Unit 3, An Island Home. This enabled the children to develop knowledge and understanding of a distant locality, working towards the learning outcome, exploring the nature and character of an environment different from their own.

A sense of place

The Cumbrian children were able to show an understanding of their sense of place through their contributions to the story. They demonstrated their ability to describe a route and to produce route maps showing some key features of the journey from home to the shops. They were also able to recognise some of the physical and human features in their locality and to reflect on the way the features were used. They talked about the ways land and buildings were used in the locality and they were aware that this was linked to the work that people did. Animals dominated their conversation as an essential part of their environment and the landscape, and they were able to name farms belonging to different family members: 'We go past your Granny's farm'. They discussed the purposes of different farm buildings and were aware of what individual buildings were used for, for example, stables, barns, farmhouses and 'Bed and Breakfasts'. They talked about the suitability of these buildings for their purpose: 'You need high stables for horses, so they can stretch their necks'. They were aware of the materials that their houses were made from, 'our house is made out of grey stone, but the porch is plastic; it's good, it keeps the rain out'. They were also able to name the sequence of shops near to the supermarket and identified the shops that they preferred to visit. Interestingly, although the children were able to discuss key features of the area in detail, no one mentioned the wind turbines which were highly visible from the school.

The children in Manchester were also able to recognise and talk about the physical and human features of their locality. They were aware of the variety of housing in the area: 'I live in a flat; it's a . . . like a square, a long house, a rectangle and it's a bit high, it's brown and red and made of bricks', 'The top of my house is a bit flat, it's made out of bricks and cement and stuck to next door', 'You get houses that are called semi-detached'. Their ability to reflect on the way some of the features from their environment were used was apparent in the discussion about shopping. They understood the functions of different shops and recognised the suitability of the buildings for different purposes: 'Asda is huge, light and long with hundreds of people', 'You get Tesco Express, they sell food, but it's not as big as Asda', 'Then you get shops like Charlie's, that's a medium shop', 'I know a little shop, it sells birthday cards, sweets, ice pops, cakes and newspapers'. The market was important for many children. They were aware that it sold a range of goods, including 'trainers, new clothes, new shoes and toys'. They recognised that some shops specialised in one type of product, 'Toys R Us just sells toys'. They were able to cite all the fast-food outlets by name, although there was some debate about whether it was 'Crunchy or Kentucky Fried Chicken'.

Children's journeys

A significant feature of the Manchester children's stories was their active participation in the journey to the shops and their attention to detail. Restricted transport in rural areas meant that all the Cumbrian children said that they would travel to the shops by car; one alternative suggestion of a quad bike was rejected as impractical. Journeys in Manchester were more varied and involved the children in walking to the shops, or walking to bus stops and waiting for the right bus: 'I get the bus because the bus stop is just outside my house. The bus is the Hazel Grove 192 bus. You have to get the right number; it says it on the front. You can't just get on any buses.'

Identifying types of transport

Some children were aware that specific types of transport were restricted to certain areas: 'You can't get a tram. That's just the city centre, but trams are good, but they cost a lot of money'. One child knew that travelling by train involved using a station.

The children in Cumbria differentiated between cars, tractors and quad bikes, but did not refer to other types of traffic. The Manchester children were keenly aware of the different forms of transport and the functions they served as is illustrated by the following observations: 'Coaches are different from buses, because they don't stop. You get school coaches, just for children, they aren't buses. You can't just get on them', 'Motorbikes go by the sides of buses in the traffic', 'Trams don't come here'. A number of children also mentioned bicycles. They were aware of logistical factors and understood that journeys cost money: 'You can go on a bus but it costs a lot of money'.

Sounds and places

When telling their stories, children were encouraged to reflect on, and include, sounds heard in their environment. Just as careful, detailed observation is important in the visual arts, careful listening is important in music. Sounds contribute to our understanding and sense of place. Places visited and journeys undertaken may inspire composers to record their impressions in sounds. They may be crucial in setting the scene for film and story.

Where sounds are heard is important. Sounds may act as pointers on a journey, indicating where we are and helping us find our way. It was therefore decided to explore how sounds suggested by children in their stories helped them make sense of their environment.

Children were invited to suggest sounds heard

- at home
- during a journey to the shops
- at the shops
- at night.

Some sounds were identified by both groups of children in their stories (wind, rain, electronic checkouts in supermarkets). However, there were marked differences. The choice of sounds by the Cumbrian children overwhelmingly reflected the

Home
- chicken crow (farmyard)
- puppy barking at kitten (farmyard)
- calm peaceful music (house/kitchen)

Journey
- jackdaws, crows, heron, cows, sheep (fields)
- goldfinches (hedges)
- woodpecker (tree)

The shops
- people talking
- trolleys
- bar-code readers
- electronic tills
- bread wrappers 'like a crushed brown leaf'

Outside shops
- busker playing guitar

Night noises
- owls (trees)
- cows (fields)
- horse sneezing (stable)
- peaceful music (in sitting room)
- boiling kettle (kitchen)
- dog hitting and scratching door (kitchen)

FIGURE 9.1　Sounds identified by children in Cumbria and built into their musical story

Home
- opening curtains
- aeroplane
- wind
- rain
- bike crashing into a lamppost
- '*Busted*' playing on radio

Journey
- car tyres in rain
- motorbikes, buses, taxis and trams
- people talking loudly on the bus
- people running/walking quickly in the street (if you open the window)

Shops
- electronic tills
- people talking/asking prices
- chips frying in the café
- fruit falling down and toys falling down when children touch them and children getting told off
- supermarket freezers
- opening drink cans (shhhhh)
- doors that open by themselves, they make a noise.
- supermarket trolley moving between aisles in supermarket
- African musicians
- trumpet player

Night noises
- mum talking
- a party
- brother talking next to him
- television

FIGURE 9.2   Sounds identified by children in Manchester and built into their musical story

presence of animals and birds in the home and rural environment. The sounds chosen by children in Manchester were dominated by sounds associated with people and transport. Both groups of sounds were described with remarkable precision. For example, a Cumbrian child's description of a horse sneezing, a Manchester child's description of car tyres on wet tarmac.

The ability to identify different sounds and to use these expressively to illustrate a story is an important milestone in children's creation and development of musical ideas at Key Stage 1 (DfEE/QCA 2000c, KS1 Music Unit 2: Sounds Interesting). Opportunities for this arose through the journey and the visit to the supermarket.

The journey

In Cumbria, children focused particularly on birdsong heard on their journey to the shops. This led to spontaneous vocal imitations. Because birds were often hidden from sight (for example, goldfinches in hedges), songs and calls of birds seemed especially important.

Children explored voices and instruments to create their own 'birdsong' composition and performance, featuring birds identified in the story. They discussed how best to re-create the sounds of familiar birds, and thought that, if possible, actual recordings of birdsong should be included in the performance. Failing this, they thought good vocal imitations were often effective. Instruments were considered fun to play, but were thought to be the least successful option – although one child's suggestion that a woodpecker might be imitated by a woodblock played with short, fast strokes was met with general approval. No one was sure what sound a heron made, but one child thought the beating of the great wings might be suggested by wafting a large piece of card to and fro.

Children again considered their journey to the supermarket on the outskirts of Kendal, identifying possible locations where birdsong and other key sounds might be heard. These places were recorded on the interactive whiteboard in the form of a simple journey map, and children developed their own symbols to represent their sound or group of sounds. A 'conductor' traced the journey of a car. As this approached agreed locations individuals or groups created birdsong, calls or sounds associated with that place.

Night noises

The Cumbrian children suggested sounds heard in the immediate vicinity and at various distances. A landscape painter develops techniques to represent features nearby and at a distance. Some sounds may be prominent and insistent; others may fade away, while others grow louder. Natural and man-made sounds in an environment can be recalled through a soundscape, or 'sound painting'. Like a landscape, a soundscape may be selective or idealised.

The soundscape presented opportunities for:

■ discussing sound qualities;

■ creating a simple musical score.

Children identified the sounds they had suggested as

■ continuous, repeated or occasional;

■ long/short/longer/shorter; loud/quiet, louder/quieter (DfEE/QCA 2000c, KS1 Music Unit 3: The long and the short of it).

The children identified the 'peaceful music' as continuous. Two children suggested that the music would sound louder when the sitting room door opened. A kettle boiling was identified as a long sound. This changed over time, starting quietly and becoming louder. The sound began with a 'click' as the kettle was switched on, ending with another click as the kettle switched off.

The soundscape was frequently punctuated by the sound of the dog 'hitting and scratching' the kitchen door. Children thought a scraping sound on a rasp or guiro might suggest scratching; perhaps a drum for repeated blows to the door.

Discussion had arisen during children's invention of the story concerning how the sound of a horse sneezing could be represented. After much debate, it was decided that this was a short, sudden sound, best created vocally.

Children considered the sounds of owls very carefully. Owls didn't call 'Too-wit too-woo'. They screamed 'like ghosts'. Toy microphones with reverberation properties provided opportunities to explore these sounds.

Supermarket

The Manchester children had suggested a wide variety of sounds associated with a large supermarket, and had described these with remarkable accuracy. They went on to develop a musical composition based on the trip to a supermarket.

The children began by reviewing their sounds and discussing ways of representing these with instruments and voices. Percussion instruments were made available, along with an electronic keyboard equipped with a number of sound effects. One girl offered a remarkable interpretation of the sound of a supermarket trolley. This involved a complex percussive/vocal imitation of wheels trundling rhythmically along. Her associated movements as the trolley veered from aisle to aisle inspired an idea for the structure of the composition. A shopper pushing a supermarket trolley would be the conductor (the identity of this key person was obvious). As she wheeled her shopping along, the sounds of 'trolley music' would be heard. As she approached the supermarket café, the sound of frying chips would be heard. On passing a group of shoppers checking out prices, a vocal call-and-response was performed.

All:	How much is it?
Shopper 1:	Five pounds fifty.
All:	How much is it?
Shopper 2:	Two pounds twenty . . .

Children explored a range of percussion and electronic sounds to represent the sounds of the electronic tills. The composition was to undergo further developments. Children decided to begin and end the composition with the opening and closing of the automatic doors. Further episodes would feature the sounds of freezers, and include a short comic 'sound story' about children upsetting a pile of fruit.

Another story: an African dimension

Giving the same story framework to an African storyteller introduced the concept of comparison with a distant locality. The storyteller agreed to produce an urban and a rural African story to ensure that the children would be able to compare like with like.

Collaborative discussion supporting the telling of the story provided the Cumbrian children with many details of features of the route. Each child added to the discussion and built on the ideas of other children. The activity illustrated the assertion that the key questions in geography link to basic literacy skills (Lewis 2004: 152). In particular, the activity addressed the first three of the sequence of 'key' questions in geography used as a structural framework by QCA. Figure 9.3 is adapted for Key Stage 1 from a framework devised by Lewis (2004: 152).

Although the shared story focused on the first three questions of the enquiry sequence, involving recognition and description of features, rather than explanation and hypothesis, several children were willing to make evaluative responses to the landscape on occasions. One child observed 'You see Whinfell every day of your life; it's good seeing it.' Another child was pleased that a new sports shop had been sited near to the supermarket: 'I'm glad JJB Sports is there. You can get a football when you go to Morrisons'. Lewis points out that although the enquiry sequence is

Key question	Concept	Language skills
What is it?	Naming and identifying	. . . physical, human and environmental features, through direct experience, story and information books.
Where is it?	Locating places and features	. . . using prepositions of place (e.g. under, through, over) learned through direct experiences and discussing pictures.
What is it like?	Describing and comparing	. . . developing descriptive language in response to visual and other senses.
How did it come to be like this?	Explaining	. . . using geographical factors to explain, recognising that there may be alternative answers and using probability words (perhaps, maybe).
How is it changing and what might happen next?	Hypothesising and predicting	Consider how a place may change. This may be through role-play or storytelling.
How do I feel about it?	Evaluating, expressing opinion and caring	Expressing feelings about possible changes, possibly through music, poetry.

FIGURE 9.3   Links between key questions in geography, key concepts and language skills (adapted for Key Stage 1 from Lewis 2004: 152)

progressive, 'It is worth noting that the final question in the sequence does not necessarily demand a higher level of thinking, for it demands an evaluative response and this can be attempted even by the very youngest learner' (Lewis 2004: 152).

Literacy links

There appeared to be clear links between geographical awareness of a sense of place and the literacy objectives relating to a growing awareness of story settings. It seemed possible to extend the literacy links envisaged by QCA in Units 1 and 3. The activities resulting from the collaborative storytelling are outlined in Figure 9.4.

Multi-sensory dimensions

In order to extend children's awareness of setting, the sessions reflected aspects of Bowkett's work on accelerated learning 'senses'. Bowkett considers that creative thinking can be promoted by stimulating skills in observation. He advocates the development of a multi-sensory approach regardless of preferred learning styles, 'although our predominant representational system may be visual, auditory or kinaesthetic, the subconscious map of reality assimilates information in a

Geography	Yr 1 QCA Unit 1	Yr 2 QCA Unit 3
	(long unit) Around our school – the local area	(short unit) An island home
	understand the variety of features that form part of their local area	identify types of transport
	understand the part people play in developing and changing the area	identify how land and buildings are used
		understand that the world extends outside their locality
Literacy	Yr 1 term 1 text level 5 describe story settings and incidents and relate them to your own experience and others	Yr 2 term 3 text level 8 compare and contrast stories with a variety of settings
	Yr 1 term 1 word level 12 Vocabulary extension	
	Yr 1 term 3 text level 14 Write stories using simple settings	
Music	Yr 1&2 QCA Unit 3 Listen carefully and identify sounds/make a soundmap showing different sounds	Yr 1&2 QCA Unit 3 Develop children's ability to discriminate longer/shorter sounds . . . create interesting sequences of sounds

FIGURE 9.4 Figure showing how links between QCA geography, literacy and music Study Units underpinned the project

multisensory way' (Bowkett 2001: 28). He advocates 'enhancing children's skill in absorbing and expressing ideas across the range of their senses'. Children were encouraged to reflect on the multi-sensory nature of their experiences of the environment. The children were very responsive to activities involving visualisation. Initial descriptions of their environment were greatly enhanced by this, and they were happy to incorporate references to the senses into the details they provided. Subsequent musical work extended auditory work. One child showed considerable interest in kinaesthetic images, describing the touching of the wrapper on a loaf of bread as being like 'crushing an old brown leaf'.

While the framework of the story was very simple, it was deliberately written to allow children to make their own responses to the text and to make the story their own. Marriott (1995: 88) notes that, 'making it possible for children to interact with texts more effectively and thus construct meanings more skilfully, enables them to learn a little more about themselves and others and the world in which they live'. The shared story sessions included opportunities for visualisation, encouraging children to close their eyes and create mental images of features in their environment. 'One of the most important ways in which texts work is to enable the reader to construct mental pictures . . . to see in our mind's eye what is happening as if we were actually participating or observing' (Marriott 1995: 86).

The most detailed aspects of the description of the landscape resulted from these opportunities to visualise and describe the images. In the Cumbrian setting, one child in Year 1 described goldfinches in the hedges and noted there might be a heron in the field. Another child described the dry stone walls by the roadside as 'walls made out of rocks'. The farm buildings were described as 'grey and old'.

In both settings it was felt that the children were able to explore the themes identified in QCA Geography long Unit 1 and to demonstrate their understanding of 'the variety of features that form part of their local area' and, to some extent 'the part people play in developing and changing the area' (QCA Unit 1). They were also able to develop the geographical vocabulary featured in this Unit.

Extending stories and localities

The introduction of the African storyteller and musician enhanced and extended the dimension of the project by providing opportunities:

- to counter misinformation and stereotypical views;
- for a creative exploration of distant localities;
- for a multi-sensory exploration of setting;
- to focus on similarities and differences.

It was felt that the introduction of a distant location would help both sets of children to develop knowledge and understanding of places outlined in QCA Unit 3, to describe what places are like and to compare places. There was an added dimension in the Manchester setting in that several of the children were of African origin. These children especially identified positively with the session and were keen to contribute to the story.

An ethical dimension

This element of the project provided the ethical and aesthetic dimensions of geographical enquiry which are discussed in Chapter 2. Walker (2004: 195) observes that 'young children are fascinated from an early age by places that are unfamiliar and distant', but warns that their ideas may reflect inaccuracies and stereotypes. Young (2004: 218) emphasises the importance of children learning about unfamiliar people and places. She stresses the significance of educators understanding the potential misunderstandings and assumptions that can 'lead to stereotyping of individuals or whole nations', resulting in mistrust and intolerance.

A discussion with the Cumbrian children revealed an ethical dilemma. Famine had been discussed as part of their work for harvest festival. They were aware that there was famine in parts of Africa and felt strongly about this. Their response was appropriate and empathetic. They had, however, over generalised. They were surprised when it was suggested that their story could be set in an African country. They insisted that it might not be possible to buy a present in Africa. They thought that all the houses would be made in the same way and that there would be no towns.

Similarities and differences

The inclusion of a distant locality provided the opportunity to address stereotyping and incorporate four of Young's ten strategies to promote the global dimension in geography (Young 2004: 221). She stresses the importance, firstly, of giving an all round view of a place or country to avoid the reinforcement of incorrect assumptions. Secondly she warns us not to generalise, because generalisations remove individuality and can be countered by focusing on particular individuals and exceptions. Thirdly, we should look for similarities before differences, because to look at similarities is to stress our common humanity and promote empathy. Her fourth point is the importance of comparing like with like and in making comparisons to stick to urban or rural scenes.

In order to compare like with like it was decided to use the story framework to produce two contrasting African stories. A rural version of the story was set in a village location in Nasarawa state, Nigeria, the shopping trip taking place in the nearby market town of Keffi. This provided an appropriate location for comparison for the children from rural Cumbria. A contrasting urban version was set in the city of Bo in Sierra Leone. Both sets of children were shown pictures from the internet to support their understanding of the localities.

QCA Geography Unit 3 identifies clear links with literacy. The children were able to develop an understanding of setting, and the impact of setting on events in a story and on the behaviour of characters. As the children moved from their familiar settings to the distant locations of Sierra Leone and Nigeria, they were able to identify similarities and differences. An accompanying photo display on interactive whiteboard supported their understanding. The Cumbrian children were interested to discover that the story was set on a farm, and were interested in photographs of village cattle that seemed very different from their own. They were also intrigued by the idea of sugar cane farms. Both groups of children responded enthusiastically as they recognised pictures of fruits mentioned in the story. The urban story highlighted common features in cities, but focused on specific differences such as the importance of water sellers in the streets, goods being sold on streets, and loud and pervasive music from speakers outside shops. In both settings it was felt that the introduction of the African stories supported children to achieve the learning objective to understand 'that the world extends outside their locality and to recognise similarities and differences' (DfEE/QCA 2000b, Unit 3).

Sense of place and story are central to children's developing understanding of the world. We were struck by the ability of young children to make detailed observations of their environments. As Marriott (1995: 87) comments, 'It is this interplay between what we know about the physical, social and emotional world and the interpretation of it presented in a story that is one of the fundamental ways in which we construct meaning.' Geography, in Key Stage 1, lies at the heart of this process.

References

Bowkett, S. (2001) *Accelerated Learning in Primary Schools (ALPS) Story Maker: Using Fiction as a Resource for Accelerated Learning*. Stafford: Network Educational Press.

DfEE/QCA (2000a) *Curriculum Guidance for the Foundation Stage*. London: DfEE/QCA.

DfEE/QCA (2000b) *Geography: A Scheme of Work for Key Stages 1 and 2 update*. London: DfEE/QCA.

DfEE/QCA (2000c) *Music: A Scheme of Work for Key Stages 1 and 2*. London: DfEE/QCA.

Goodwin, D. and Perkins, M. (1998) *Teaching Language and Literacy in the Early Years*. London: David Fulton Publishers.

Lewis, L. (2004) 'Geography and language development', in Scoffham, S. (ed.) *Primary Geography Handbook*. Sheffield: Geographical Association.

Marriott, S. (1995) *Read On: Using Fiction in the Primary School*. London: Paul Chapman Publishing.

Martin, F. and Owens, P. (2004) 'Young children making sense of their place in the world', in Scoffham, S. (ed.) *Primary Geography Handbook*. Sheffield: Geographical Association.

Walker, G. (2004) 'Contrasting localities', in Scoffham, S. (ed.) *Primary Geography Handbook*. Sheffield: Geographical Association.

Wells, G. (1987) *The Meaning Makers: Children Learning to Use Language and Using Language to Learn*. London: Hodder and Stoughton.

Young, M. (2004) 'Geography and the global dimension', in Scoffham, S. (ed.) *Primary Geography Handbook*. Sheffield: Geographical Association.

How can geography have a significant place in a restructured Key Stage 2 curriculum?

Hilary Cooper

Excellence and Enjoyment: A Strategy for Primary Schools (DfES 2003) and the 'Futures' programme (QCA 2005) aim to address the fragmented and overloaded curriculum which has developed over the past 15 years, by encouraging teachers to be responsible for constructing a more integrated, meaningful, creative curriculum. This can encompass both the benefits of the National Curriculum and a holistic approach to child development, but requires some careful restructuring. This chapter discusses first, ways in which core values and key skills can be developed through geographical concepts, then how geography can be linked to other subjects.

Core values at the heart of geographical concepts

Key concepts developed in geography include: diversity, interdependence, pattern, process, community, change, location and sustainability. Each of these involves sub-concepts which can often be linked to the core values underpinning the curriculum. For example, the concept of diversity includes looking at similarities and differences, which in turn relates closely to the core value of tolerance. The Plowden Report (Plowden 1967) emphasised that a school is not merely a teaching shop; it must transmit values and attitudes. Now these values have been defined. 'Foremost is a belief in education . . . as a route to spiritual, moral, social, cultural and physical education . . . and thus the wellbeing of each individual' (DfEE/QCA1999: 10–13). We need to explore ways in which these dimensions, themselves interdependent, can also be made integral to the curriculum.

Spiritual development: a sense of place

The concept of 'spiritual' is complex and problematic. Halstead defines education of the human spirit as involving both internal spiritual identity and a spiritual response to life (Halstead 1997: 99). Spiritual development includes pupils developing 'curiosity about themselves and their place in the world, as they try to answer for themselves some of life's fundamental questions' (DfEE/QCA 1999: 19). Scoffham (2004: 9) acknowledges that geography focuses on values and has a strong spiritual dimension. Boxer and Walker (2005) explain how, as children talk about places that are special to them, why and what it feels like to be there, they are 'sharing something of their inner self' (NC Geography, KS2: 1a; 3a–f) (DES/WO 1990). They are developing the ability to reflect on what is its importance to them and to others, deepening their own sense of themselves and of their own place in the wider community. There are many aspects of geography which encourage spiritual development. Places and their significance to us form the basis of much of the development of concepts associated with the sense of awe and wonder. (Beauty and aesthetic appreciation and the development of enquiries are explored in Chapters 2 and 3. The development of geographical concepts of place, further explored through art, music and literature, is discussed below.)

Moral development: interdependence, community, sustainability

'Moral development involves acquiring an understanding of the difference between right and wrong, a concern for others and the will to do what is right' (DfEE/QCA 1999: 19). Moral development depends on the opportunities children are given to reason about and discuss ethical dilemmas in increasingly complex ways. Barnes (2004: 28) points out that as children become aware of the interdependence of people around the world and within our complex multicultural society, they become increasingly aware that what is 'true' or 'right' for some people may not be the same for all people. Geography provides many dilemmas involving moral conflict, local, national and global (NC Geography, KS2: 1b–e; 6c–e) (DES/WO 1990). To investigate issues children will need to first find out who are the stakeholders, who has the power to make changes and who can influence the decision-makers (NC Geography, KS2: 2g) (Jackson 2004). This can often be done through the use of fiction, where the issues can be discussed in a common context and without the sensitivity that surrounds most moral issues in the subject. The question, 'Should our high street be closed to traffic?', might be better discussed in the context of a story like *Adam and Paradise Island* (Keeping 1989). A 'philosophy for children' approach (discussed in Chapters 2 and 7) is another way of addressing moral issues in the teaching and learning of geography. The approach emphasises thinking skills, speaking and listening, collaborative learning, emotional literacy and values education. Children can create thoughtful questions and enquire into them with others; this has been shown to develop self-esteem and, because the questions come from the children, promotes curiosity and 'learning to learn'. At the same time, this approach introduces a number of challenges for the teacher, particularly in planning, since the approach depends upon children asking the questions. Chapters 2 and 3 explore some of these dilemmas.

Concepts in geography where moral development is particularly central include interdependence, community and sustainability. There are many opportunities for developing these, an example being The British Empire and Commonwealth Museum in Bristol. This museum provides rich opportunities for primary school children to explore moral issues; human rights in Africa and the Carribean, immigration and racism in Britain, fair trade in Ghana, the environment. In groups they present reports of their research which are broadcast locally for a month each year on Commonwealth FM.

Personal and social development: awareness of diversity

'Social development involves acquiring an understanding of the responsibilities and rights of being members of families and communities (local, national, global)' (DfEE/QCA 1999: 20). It involves emotional intelligence: the ability to understand one's emotions in order to empathise with others and to express emotion in productive ways (Goleman 1996). Geography raises children's awareness of and understanding of diversity, of the variety of human conditions and of caring for the earth and its peoples (NC Geography, KS2: 3) (DES/WO 1990: 6). It also helps children to understand their often powerful feelings about different places, to express them verbally or through art, photography, music, to use this understanding to inform responses to environmental issues and to accept that others may feel differently about a place (NC Geography, KS2: 5a,b).

The Citizenship curriculum aims to develop personal and social skills, knowledge, understanding and attitudes that make an active contribution to the democratic process. The enhanced profile of Education for Sustainable Development encourages pupils to participate in decisions about the way we do things, individually and collectively, locally and globally (NC Geography, KS2: 5); this too is a dimension of personal and social development. Good practice can be found in schools that have made these connections and particularly in primary schools where teachers are more used to working across a range of subjects (Iwaskow 2005).

Cultural development: celebrating diversity

This involves pupils developing an understanding of their own culture, including a variety of aesthetic experiences and an interest in others' diverse ways of doing things (DfEE/QCA 1999: 20). Geography investigates the relationships between physical environments, climates and their effects on the lives of the people who live in them and vice versa (on their homes, their work, their leisure, and their art, literature and music). It explores the causes and impacts of these changes on people's lives and the communications between communities, local, national and global (NC Geog-raphy, KS2: 1, 3). At Key Stage 2 children make these comparisons, both between places in the United Kingdom and in Europe and the wider world. Conceptually making comparisons raises a number of complex issues, not least the difficulty of comparing places which we have experienced and places that we have not experienced (see Chapter 5 for further discussion of this). Often awareness of other cultures is more important than comparison and geography can play an important role in the cultural development of pupils. Harrow Local Education Authority is developing a 'Countries of Origin' project to promote greater understanding of the cultural traditions of the 60 per cent of Harrow pupils, many of them third generation, who come from ethnic minorities, and build these traditions into the daily life of schools. For example, children who are comparing localities in London and in a city in India might go on, in narrative writing, to draw on Indian and African storytelling traditions (Barnard 2005: 6–7). Teachers in Harrow have already undertaken exchange visits and it is hoped that later there will be long-term exchanges between teachers, social workers, researchers and pupils. Chris McDermott, a middle school head teacher who has been on an exchange to India, sees the project as part of the vision for the world of work and life in the twenty-first century, as well as for any ethical and moral considerations. Partington Primary School, in Trafford, is linked with schools in Uganda and in Paris. Children of all ages write to each other. The head teacher sees links with the Ugandan school as supplementing geography, work on the environment and in science, while the French school, with which they celebrate European Culture Week, also helps with teaching French (Lepkowska 2005: 17).

Joan Dickie, a Norfolk head teacher, is a veteran of Comenius European partnerships. 'The children find it very motivating,' she says, 'to know that their work will be touched, displayed and enjoyed by children in another country. They are also fascinated by their counterparts' daily lives – in particular what they have in common.' She suggests teachers find partnership schools by accessing the Comenius website in order to find out how to attend contact seminars, or by looking on Partbase or Global Gateway for Comenius partners. There is funding available for preparatory visits for Comenius School Development projects. These involve at least three partners and last for up to three years. The projects are cross-curricular (Thomas 2005: 22). The focus of such links is the similarities between humans rather than differences. When, as part of a project organised by the Save the Children Fund, children across the world were asked to draw and exchange pictures illustrating their first day at school, they showed that, from their first day, they began to learn about the developing world and found economic differences but many similarities too. In schools in Pakistan and in Somerset 'children drew themselves in the same way', 'circular faces and triangular dresses and hair rising in gravity-defying u-bends!' (Bloom 2005: 12).

Citizenship: community and change

Awareness of similarities and differences between places, whether local, national or global, raises questions of morality and responsible citizenship: the relationship between developed and less developed countries, environmental issues and sustainable development, responses to natural disasters and international events. The key concept that geography considers in relation to citizenship is probably that of community. What makes a community and what contributes to a community can be considered in a number of ways.

Year 5 pupils at the National Junior School in Grantham undertook fieldwork relating to concepts of change: proposals to pedestrianise the High Street (NC Geography KS2: 1, 2, 5). They recorded land use, discussed possible futures for a vacant building, giving reasons for their choices, and considered effects of pedestrianisation on all sectors of the community (Akester *et al.* 2005). Rowley and Lewis (2003) describe a fascinating project on environmental education and citizenship in which primary children raise and discuss a rich variety of questions relevant to the locality, for example, how do we decide where it is suitable to place a wind turbine? In both examples the concept of community is constantly revisited in the process of considering how decisions are made.

At Canon Burrows CE Primary School, Oldham, an ECO group ensures that there is a lively response from the pupils to school and local environmental issues the children care about and uses a similar 'critical thinking' approach to 'big issues' such as human rights, global pollution, war and peace, poverty (NC Geography, KS2: 1–5). Children discuss key questions in their classes so that they can develop the themes for assemblies (www.qca.org.uk/geography).

Schools link with the wider community in a variety of ways. One Suffolk school has an email link with a school in Skye and has also established links with Papua New Guinea over deforestation, through the Green Light Trust (www.greenlight-trust.org). Year 6 in a Hampshire primary school have argued about the causes and prevention of global warming, while Year 5 argued about the needs for identity cards, as part of a Europe unit (NC Geography, KS2: 5).

As for the human dimensions of natural disasters, Swift and Lambert (2005: 22) say that there is no 'right' way to teach about these but that, in order to help young citizens think rationally about such events, we need to 'call on their geographical thinking in a sustained way'; one-off sequences of lessons representing, for example, the tsunami, with an emphasis on sympathy for the victims, may be inappropriate. They say that geography's key concept that guides our choices in how to cover such an event is interdependence. 'None of the places affected, directly, or indirectly, by the event is isolated. There is a complex web of physical, human and environmental processes that connects us all. Children need to connect their learning about this event with their work related to other natural events and the impact of human processes' (NC Geography, KS2: 4). In Chapter 3 John Goodwin suggests how time may be managed to respond to such events.

Thinking skills: knowing how to learn

Key transferable skills are central to a value-laden and enquiry-based approach to geography. The following is a case study identifying thinking skills and key skills developed through a geography project.

Year 5 children in Budleigh Salterton were shown a newspaper article 'Summer holiday Shackletons put Antarctica in peril' (Tremlett 2003) to explore as a geographical and environmental issue, 'Should Antarctic tourism be limited?' (Mackintosh 2005), (QCA 2000, Scheme of Work 16: What's in the News?). Skills, like values, are not discrete but the analyses in Figures 10.1 and 10.2 illustrate the range of thinking and communication skills developed through one short topic and the inclusive approach of the emphasis on oracy.

Information processing skills	Extract information about views of different people from newspaper article and photograph. Extract evidence to support arguments from different perspectives from the internet, other photos, and brochures. Use information from globes, maps, atlases.
Reasoning skills	Develop arguments, supported by evidence, from point of view of tourists, tour operators, explorers, environmentalists, shipping companies, scientists, wild life. Weigh arguments.
Enquiry skills	Identify issue – express in own words. Identify and investigate key questions using geographical skills and concepts: Where is it taking place? What is the place like? How could we get there?
Creative thinking skills	Use imagination to see issue from different perspectives.
Evaluation skills	Consider what is important. Understand the need to reach a consensus in a group, to show tolerance, and compromise. Class debate, followed by need to reach a point of view. Evaluate tour company's video for bias.

FIGURE 10.1 Analysis of thinking skills developed through the enquiry, 'Should Antarctic tourism be limited?' (Mackintosh 2005)

Communication skills	Express opinions and listen to others. Discussion. Debate. Persuasive posters. Persuasive letters, making points confidently and politely. How to sell ideas (as a tour company). Use of specialised vocabulary (e.g. Southern hemisphere, South Pole) and specialised concepts (inter-connectedness, sustainability, reversibility, management; similarity/difference; change, causes, effects).
Application of number	Use maps, brochures and timetables to plan routes to Antarctica, taking into account distance, cost and time, justifying choice.
Information technology	Information from the internet, video. Make posters, write letters.
Working with others	Small group discussion. Class debate.
Improving own learning and performance	Role-play radio discussion modelled by teachers. Evaluate tourist video and realise being manipulated.
Problem-solving	Identifying a problem and suggesting and evaluating possible responses.

FIGURE 10.2 Analysis of key generic skills involved in the enquiry, 'Should Antarctic tourism be limited? (Mackintosh 2005)

Geography Plus: a case study integrating core values

An afternoon at Langdale School, a two class school in Cumbria, illustrated ways in which core values and thinking skills embedded in geography can extend beyond the planned geography topics which are taught at Key Stage 2 during alternate terms, for one afternoon a week, by a specialist part-time teacher. 'This ensures that the children have a basic geographical framework,' the head teacher explained. But everywhere I looked there was evidence of geography also integrated flexibly within a variety of cross-curricular projects. One had originated from the children, one by a parent, one by the head teacher and one as part of work with a resident photographic artist. 'We drip-feed aspects of geography into other projects as they arise,' the head teacher said. Always, the characterising features were that much of the organisation was done by the children. There was an emphasis on 'what is real', on making connections and on involving parents and the community.

Earthkeepers: a spiritual dimension

One day William had remarked that there was 'a lot of rubbish' on the school field; the rest of the children were also concerned. Not long afterwards a letter arrived from a mysterious 'E.M.', inviting them to join 'The Earthkeepers'. Three keys (of knowledge, experience and knowing yourself) had to be earned before the secret meaning of mysterious E.M. would be revealed. The children were sent diaries and tasks to perform, requiring parents' signatures to confirm that they had been achieved. Tasks had a spiritual dimension; finding a magic spot and spending time there at least once a week for a month; exploring a new natural area and spending two hours getting immersed in it on two occasions, listening to sounds and discovering natural treasures; recording thoughts and feelings about these tasks in a diary, and writing a story or poem about them each week for four weeks. The display board revealed wonderful photographs of 'magic spots', with explanations. One read, 'We drew down the veil of silence. We had a perfect view of the reservoir. A magic spot is where you can sit quietly alone.'

Resident photographic artist: changing communities

This focus was on photography of the local quarry. However, explaining the photographs, and what the children had learned from interviews with people who had worked in the quarry long ago, involved many literacy objectives associated with non-chronological writing, explanatory diagrams, and ways of organising information. The geography strand lay in describing the place, using maps and photographs, finding out how it came to be as it was, recording evidence about the quarry and its impact on the community. The children recorded changes in the landscape, using geographical vocabulary (NC Geography, KS2: 2, 3; NC History KS2: 3).

An art workshop

During a walk in the National Park children described and recorded their environment as sketches: woods, streams, farm buildings, mountains. They collected feathers, stones, wood, leaves and mosses. Back at school they sensitively and thoughtfully 'breathed new life into them', in the tradition of Kurt Schwitters, who had made similar collages in this area in the 1940s, by incorporating them into their drawings (NC Geography, KS2. 1a, b, e; NC Art, KS2: 1a–c, 2a–c, 4a,c).

Sandipani Muni School, Vrindavan: understanding cultural diversity

When three of the children and their parents went on holiday to India they made contact with a school for street children. The head teacher of Sandipani Muni School sent Langdale children her school's prospectus, photographs of the school, a group photograph of all the pupils, children in their classrooms, children's drawings and – the oxen-drawn school bus. The Langdale children took their own photographs and selected the ones to send, after much discussion. They exchanged hand-made cards (NC Geography, KS2: 1). Those from Sandipani were not, at first glance, different from the Cumbrian cards, asking 'How are you?' and 'Are you well?' But the pictures were of palm trees, tropical fruits, clay lamps. This is just the beginning of developing understanding of cultural diversity.

Manchester exchange: 'We see flats, they see mountains' – interdependence

This was the heading in the *Times Educational Supplement* (13 February 2004) describing an exchange between the Langdale children and Year 6 children in an inner-city Manchester school of 400 children. Children from both schools first exchanged letters telling their partners a little about themselves and where they lived. Then the Manchester school came to stay in the nearby outdoor education centre for a week. Children from both schools, in mixed groups of six, were taught climbing skills. 'Finding my friend from the letters was fantastic,' said William. 'He helped me in the difficult places.' Then the Langdale children went to school in Manchester – an amazing experience. Innocent racist comments had to be addressed in some real situations. Questions about different cultures arose. 'Why are they not eating anything?' was a first contact with Ramadan and maybe dawning realisation of concepts of interdependence (NC Geography, KS2: 3). Langdale may be a small rural school but the 'drip-feed' approach to Geography Plus means that they have rich and broad direct experiences of other people and places. The Manchester Langdale Exchange was funded by the Countryside Agency, Cumbria Youth Alliance and the Access and Conservation Trust.

The following is a case study with a geography focus integrating core values and cross-curricular links.

I entered Year 4's classroom at Eaglesfield Paddle School through an arch of Indian fabric sparkling with mirrors, and embroidery of flowers, leaves and birds. Indian fabric was draped around the walls. On the table were Indian artefacts: a reading stand, a velvet and sequined box, a carved elephant, models of Hindu gods. I was surrounded by 'Images of Chembakolli' (QCA 2000, Geography Scheme Unit 10). There were children's paintings based on, for example, photographs of the valley of Chembakolli, and of the Chembakolli tree with its beautiful white flowers, surrounding tea plantations, paintings of the blue mountains of the Nilgiri Hills in Tamil Nadu. 'We are having some "India days" next week,' the teacher, Cath Lawler, explained. 'Would you like to come?'

India day

When I arrived on an 'India Day', there were four rotating group activities. One group was making chicken curry, nan bread, and kheere ka raita; there was a pungent smell of garlic being crushed with ginger, onions being chopped and of gently cooking turmeric, chilli powder, cumin and cardamom. The cooks were discussing the food, how and why it is different from traditional English food.

In one group, children were tie-dying squares of cotton, and talking about natural dyes. In another they designed and embroidered 'Indian leaf designs' with a liberal application of sequins, and discussed how the lotus leaf pattern had been transformed into Paisley in the cotton factories of nineteenth-century Scotland, although not how the English monopolies in the nineteenth century had destroyed the Indian cotton industry. The fourth group were making shadow puppets to tell the story of Rama and Sita. They had already had an Indian dance afternoon led by the music adviser.

Interviews

Celebrating diversity

I was interested in talking to the children about the Chembakolli project. They suggested I might like to interview them since I had my camcorder with me. They left the classroom in small groups. Each group had a camera person so that I could join in the spontaneous discussion. And they had some interesting things to tell me. First, the topic seemed to have encouraged confidence and curiosity! No Asians lived in this rural area but Ben had met an Indian, who was a Hindu. 'Where?' 'In Lanzerotti.' 'How do you know he was a Hindu?' 'It was a she. I asked her.'

The children told me that they knew a little about India before the Chembakolli project, from television. They talked about elephants and curry but 'You get more ideas from school.' 'There are a lot of poor people there. They have to go down to the river to get water and they haven't got much money.'

'I didn't know they picked so many tea leaves. I thought tea came from a sort of vine.' 'I didn't think the estates would be so big.' 'It's a global market.'

'I didn't know they made honey, – to sell it. In Chembakolli there's someone called Honey Patel! – No, it probably doesn't come from hives. I'm only guessing here but I think they get it from climbing rocks . . . I saw a television programme about it.'

The children also seemed to have picked up some different social and cultural values. 'All the money they earn goes between them. The women may buy cloth, – and books for the children and some is for seeds' – and so on. 'I learned this from some leaflets we were reading.'

'They don't cut down trees but they grow plants around trees.' 'It's to get a balance.' 'They say that they work with nature.'

Conclusion of an India day

When I returned from the interviews, the cooking group were settling down to their curry. Those who had been sceptical were urged to, 'try a little bit'. Before long everyone was eating with enthusiasm – including Cath and me.

The tie-dye cotton squares were drying and the embroidery tidied away. Downstairs the shadow puppet play was being performed from behind a back-lighted puppet theatre, to an enthusiastic audience booing and cheering in all the right places.

Cross-curricular links: different ways of learning about places

The theory of multiple intelligences (Gardner 1993) emphasises the many ways in which different children may explore new knowledge and concepts. For example, Jerome Monahan (2005: 30) describes a Year 3 project based on a visit to a beach, which mixes history, geography and science. However, it is essential that key skills, concepts and understanding at the centre of each subject, are identified in planning, in order to build on the developments created by the National Curriculum and avoid a return to topics as a rag-bag of activities connected only by content.

Geography and mathematics

Many opportunities to apply mathematics to geographical enquiries as required in the National Curriculum (DfEE/QCA 1999: 67) are given in the supplementary examples of the Numeracy Strategy (DfEE 1999: 7–9, 12–13, 15, 101, 108–9, 113, 115) and in the Geography scheme for Years 1–6 Unit 25, Geography and Numbers (QCA 2000). These include: estimates, probability and measurement of distance, scale, direction, journey times, journey costs, making and interpreting bar charts and graphs of temperature, rainfall, exports, prices, wages maps, directions and grids. Margaret Mackintosh (2005) stresses the importance of analysis and explanation, using geographical thinking (www.geography.org.uk/projects/gtip/thinkpieces). Links between geography and mathematics are also given in Scoffham (2004: 55, 67, 71).

Geography and literacy

English, like mathematics and ICT, is a communication system. It was always intended that the objectives of the National Literacy Strategy (DfEE 1998) should be applied in the context of subjects, for a purpose. Every aspect of the Strategy can be applied through geography: reading and writing signs, labels, captions, non-chronological reports, observations, articles, describing and classifying, instructional texts, directions, explanations, viewpoints, differentiating between fact and opinion, discussion, debate. There are opportunities for reading and writing information text, fiction and poetry, stories accompanied by 'fictional' maps, and discussing settings for stories. Developing speaking and listening through drama in geographical contexts is explored in Chapter 5 and through story in Chapter 9.

Reading – and writing – poetry about places, features and landscape can dramatically capture the spirit of a place; young children can often enjoy an extract from an adult poem. Possibilities are endless. One useful anthology (Baker 2000) is divided into such sections: Mountains, Hills and the View from Above; Rivers and Streams; Lakes, Floods, Marshes and Fens; Sea and Coast; Moors, Heaths and Barren Places;

and Secret and Special Places. The English curriculum also includes stories and poems from a range of cultures.

Geography and ICT

Similarly ICT is a communication system which can be built into geographical enquiry: for example, organising tables, text, images and sound for multimedia presentations or desktop publishing (NC ICT, KS1, 2: 2a). Simulations and models to investigate effects of changing values (NC ICT, KS2: 2c) are particularly motivating (Richards 2005: 29). By contrast, the Ambleside School website offers a tour of the Lake District, which involves captions, free software to download and links literacy and numeracy with geography. (See also Scoffham 2004: 165–77, 308, 346.)

Geography and science

There can often be links between geography and science: Life and Living Processes, linked to conservation issues or to global health issues; Materials and Properties (NC Science, KS2: 31d), linked to describing and grouping rocks and soils, traditional clothing, building materials and changing materials to weather (freezing, evaporating).

Humanities: geography and history

History and geography often link easily, either by sequencing a history study unit with a geography unit, for example, between a local history study (NC History, KS2: 7) and a local geography study (NC Geography, KS2: 6a); the local history could be linked to the locality in Roman, Anglo-Saxon or Viking times, Tudor or Victorian times or Britain since 1930. A local history study could be integrated with a geography study of water and its effects on landscape, how settlements differ and change, or to an environmental issue (NC Geography, KS2: 6c,d,e); or a world history unit of study (NC History, KS2: 13) may be linked to the same locality today (NC Geography, KS2: 6a).

Geography and the arts

The arts can be a valuable starting point for a geographical enquiry, which can involve observing and recording in a variety of media, using a variety of genres, styles or traditions. Children should also know about the role of artists and craftspeople from different cultures and times. The starting point for children's explor-ations in a variety of media should be their experiences, music, and environments; they should investigate a variety of genres, styles and traditions, and know about the role of artists and craftspeople in different cultures and times (DfEE/QCA 1999: 120–1).

Music

> Music is landscape:
> wide grass
> melts to a skyline,
> dips to a stream.
> Landscape is music
> the heart's dream
> weaves with what we see
> and beguiles us.
>
> (Robertson 2005)

Dance and folk songs allow children to access the customs and emotions of different countries and to consider how dances have been influenced by their environments; stately folk dances in hot countries such as Spain, fast dances in Northern Europe, Hungary and Poland; songs and dances to celebrate seasons and agricultural work and patterns (NC Geography KS2: 3; NC Music KS2, 1a,3a,b,c,d). Classical music often describes landscapes and seasons: Benjamin Brittain's wonderful descriptions of the North Sea in Preludes (Peter Grimes); Vaughan Willliams' the Fenn Country, or Wenlock Edge, full of air and sky and space; Butterfield's Banks of Green Willow. Presented in a context, Key Stage 2 children are quite able to enjoy passages from such music (NC Music, KS2 : 5e) (see Figure 10.3).

Alternatively children can create music after listening to sounds in urban or rural environments, or particular places within them: a wood or a waterfall, a building site, an airport or market, or a journey between places, as they do in Chapter 9 (NC Music, KS2: 1–4).

Excellent links can be made between traditional music, dance (NC PE, KS2: 6) and stories, and cultures of other places using the website, www.tuned-in.org. For Key Stages 2 and 3, the culture of the Hausa people of West Africa is explored through text, illustrated by photographs, and music, stories, songs and dances (NC Geography, KS2: 1a–e, 3; NC Music, KS2: 1–4, NC PE, KS2: 6; NC English literature: 8a–f). For Key Stages 2 and 3 there is also traditional music from China. Each theme is intended to result in a performance.

Another approach to geography through music is described by a Warwickshire teacher whose school set up a partnership with a school in Ghana, through a website. He visited Ghana and was taught traditional local rhythms by a master drummer. 'We were playing in the shadow of a tree with the sound of dancing feet on hard earth and the dust rising around us . . . Now when I teach drumming the children are learning the oral tradition of a specific village using a drum made from a tree. It means something,' he said (Bloom 2005: 1–4), (NC Geography, KS2: 3; NC Music, KS2: 1–4). The Aklowa Centre offers the next best thing; lessons in traditional West

Countries, towns, places

United Kingdom
- *The Land of the Mountain and the Flood*: MacCunn
- 'Scottish' Symphony: Mendelssohn
- *The Hebrides*: Mendelssohn
- *Severn Suite*: Holst
- *Silent Wood*: Elgar
- *In the South*: Elgar
- 'London' Symphony: Vaughan Williams
- *Knightsbridge*: Coates
- *On Wenlock Edge*: Vaughan Williams
- *Norfolk Rhapsodies*: Vaughan Williams
- *Tintagel*: Bax

France
- French comic operas: Offenbach
- *Cris de Paris*: Jannequin
- *Paris*: Delius
- *An American in Paris*: Gershwin

Spain
- *Symphonie Espagnole*: Lalo
- *La Soirée dans Grenade* (from Estampes): Debussy
- 'Par les rues et par les chemins' (Images II): Debussy
- *Espagna*: Albeniz
- *March of the Toreadors* (*Carmen*): Bizet
- *Rhapsodie Espagnol*: Ravel
- *Espagna*: Chabrier
- *Cappriccio Espagnol*: Rimsky-Korsakov
- *Nights in the Gardens of Spain*: De Falla

Germany
- Symphony No. 3 ('Rhenish'): Schumann
- Symphony No. 38 ('Prague'): Mozart

Austria
- Symphony No. 34 ('Linz'): Mozart

Italy
- *Aus Italien*: R. Strauss
- *Harold in Italy*: Berlioz
- *Capriccio Italien*: Tchaikovsky

Hungary
- *Hungaria*: Liszt

Norway
- *Four Norwegian Moods*: Stravinsky

Finland
- *Finlandia*: Sibelius

Russia
- Russian Overture: Prokofiev
- *Russia*: Balakirev
- *The Great Gate of Kiev*: Mussorgsky
- Symphony No. 2 ('Little Russian'): Tchaikovsky

Asia
- *In the Steppes of Central Asia*: Borodin

Antarctica
- *Sinfonia Antarctica*: Vaughan Williams

South America
- *Saudades de Brazil*: Milhaud

North America
- *On the Waterfront*: Bernstein
- *America*: Bernstein
- *Florida*: Gould
- *Appalachian Spring*: Copland
- *San Francisco Polyphony*: Bernstein
- *Grand Canyon Suite*: Grofe
- *Billy the Kidd*: Copland

Dances
- Scottish/Cornish/English Dances: Arnold
- *Dances of Galanta*: Kodaly (Hungary)
- 'Farandole' (*L'Arlesienne*): Bizet
- *Can Can*: Offenbach
- *Don Quixote*: Gerhard
- Cossack Dance (Mazeppa): Tchaikovsky

Landscape
- *Helios*: Nielson
- Pastoral Symphony: Beethoven
- *Roses from the South*: Berlioz (Italy)
- *An Imaginary Landscape*: Birtwistle
- *Alpine Symphony*: Strauss
- *Men and Mountains*: Mussorgsky
- *Les Collines d'Anacapri*: Debussy (Italy)

Weather
- *Nuages*: Debussy
- Pastoral Symphony (Fourth movement – storm): Beethoven
- Thunder and Lightening Polka: Johann Strauss
- *The Tempest*: Sibelius

Seasons
- *Summer*: Bridge
- 'Summer Morning by a Lake' ('Farben') (Five pieces): Schoenberg
- Symphony No. 1 ('Spring'): Schumann
- *11 Echoes of Autumn*: Crumb
- *Winter Bonfire*: Prokofiev
- *The Seasons* (from Sicilian Vespers): Verdi
- *The Four Seasons*: Vivaldi
- *The Seasons*: Haydn

FIGURE 10.3 Indicative music of different styles which can be linked to geography

African drumming, and cooking with a journey in a traditional boat through swamps 'which may be crocodile infested' (www.aklowa.net).

Art and design

I do believe that painting can change the world. If you see the world as beautiful, thrilling and mysterious, as I do, then you feel quite alive.

(Hockney 2004: 157)

Making pictures of places, in whatever medium, allows us not only to look intensely and to focus on what interests us, but also to record a personal and emotional connection with the place. This is clear in the way a class of children will all produce dramatically personal interpretations of the same place.

Developing an understanding of places also provides rich opportunities to learn to appreciate the art of other cultures. All countries, for example, have developed their own traditional fabric designs: brightly coloured woollen fabrics of the Andes, Indian saris decorated with embroidery and glass mirrors, the traditional Adinkra cloth of Ghana, Scottish plaids. Children can try replicating the embroidery, the printing or the weaving. They can be introduced to the traditional crafts (plastic arts, pottery, ceramics) of the place they are studying and have a go at replicating them (NC Geography KS2: 3a, b; NC Art KS2: 1-5 (in particular 4c, 5d)).

Similarly they can evaluate images of urban and rural environments they study, in different styles, comparing methods and approaches, and develop their own work according to their views (DfEE/QCA 1999: 120). There are endless possibilities for comparison. Some suggestions are given in Figure 10.4.

The Tate Gallery, the National Gallery and many local galleries offer excellent support for primary school visits which meet the needs of the teacher's learning intentions. Recording and communicating places and features graphically involves making symbolic images, observing shape, pattern, colour, form, relationships between things, similarities and differences, scale, distance, size. What we select to record and how we do so reveals much about our own feelings and how we may be seeing, thinking and feeling differently from others.

An amazing internet site (www.earthgoogle.com) allows you to move between places anywhere on earth, and to zoom in on specific features and streets. Pupils have based wonderful fabric designs on the patterns which emerge from exploring this website and, as they worked, discussed the reasons for the patterns: the convergence of roads, the flow of rivers, the spread of cities (Rowley and Lewis 2003: 29).

Other sites, provide access to collections of landscapes in many styles, expressing a diversity of spatial representations. For example, the landscapes of Canada, Mexico and the United States combine religious, scientific and philosophical ideals as well as the artists' personal vision (www.virtualmuseum.ca.Exhibitions/

Technique	Environment	Referenced examples
Photographs, drawings, painting, wall hangings, embroidery, collage, clay, yarn wrapping, weaving, printing	*Rural landscape* – pond, swamp, trees, wheat field	Clement and Page (1992)
	Urban landscapes Docklands. Where town meets land Forest landscape (The main idea of this project described was to take an environment that the children thought they already knew and to look at it again through the artist's 'seeing eye')	Binch and Clive (1994)
Photographs, drawings, painting, embroidery, printing	*Small-scale environments* – hedgerows, plants, feathers, animals, stones, shells	Clement and Page (1992)
As above	Maps, bird's eye views	Clement and Page (1992) www.earthgoogle.com
Painting, ceramics, murals (Examples of questions to ask related to geography and art)	*Urban landscapes* – buildings and their uses	Binch and Clive (1994: 93–9)
■ Observing/copying in paint, weaving, embroidery, fabrics, threads, cloth for different environments, symbolism in fabrics ■ Drawing and modelling artefacts from different cultures (e.g. body adornment, architectural features) ■ Printing – how wood, metal used in different cultural contexts; different language symbols for blocks (Greek, Hindi, Chinese) ■ Tape/slide show	Art and craft from different cultures and contexts Narrative of traditional South African tale	Callaway and Kear (1999) See also Binch and Clive (1994) for topic on 'Change', part of a cultural diversity project in which children, led by a black artist, drew Benin Binch and Clive (1994)bronzes from museums, plundered from Nigeria, and 'learned how art can be a vehicle for commenting on social justice'.

FIGURE 10.4 Examples of techniques in art which can be used to explore environments

Landscapes). The Smithsonian National Museum of African Art (www.nmafa. si.edu.exhibits/) has wonderful exhibitions of ancient and modern African art; for example, Urhobo art, artefacts and ceramics, art from Benin, textiles from Madagascar and Morocco. Other useful websites are given at the end of this chapter.

British Isles
John Constable, Sheila Fell, David Hockney, L.S. Lowry, Eric Ravilious, Winifrid Nicholson, John Nash, Samuel Palmer, Dante Gabriel Rosetti, Stanley Spencer, Graham Sutherland, J.M.W. Turner, Alfred Wallis
(see, e.g., www.tate.org.uk)

European tradition
Canaletto, Corot, Veuillard, Monet, Seurat, Van Gogh, Vlaminck, Derain, Kokoschka

Non-European tradition
See www.artpromote.com/ethnic.shtml for ethic art around the world
See www. nmafa.si.edu
African art, see Smithsonian Museum of African Art
Yoruba; British Museum
Abu'l Hansan (c. 1630); British Museum
Katushika Housai; Hokasai
Aboriginal drawings
Oriental paintings
American landscapes (evolving landscape, social landscape, mythic landscape, personal landscape, see www.N.American landscape.virtualmuseum.ca

FIGURE 10.5   Examples of artists whose landscape, townscape and seascape styles can be compared and contrasted

Developing an understanding of place through art can develop cultural awareness but also spiritual and uniquely personal awareness. For the art we make, is the way we individually see the world. We see a view as being outside ourselves even though it is only a mental representation of what we experience inside. Figure 10.5 suggests starting points in exploring places and cultures through arts and crafts.

Planning for integration and coherence

If a school feels secure using modifications of the QCA schemes of work (QCA 2000), links can be planned between schemes for geography and schemes for other subjects. It is suggested by the QCA that Geography Unit 11 can be linked to Science Unit 6c, More About Dissolving, and parts of Geography Unit 13, a contrasting UK locality. Parts of Geography Unit 22 on a contrasting locality overseas can be linked with French Unit 14.

However, the model given for making links between these Units could be used imaginatively to make links between geography and other subjects. The rationale needs to be clear. There need to be common or related learning objectives, common activities and resources which best serve each subject, or complementary activities in each subject. The need for some separate lessons also needs to be identified, as

Subject	Scheme	Geography scheme links	Possible links to other subjects
Science	3D. Rocks and soils (Y3)	Unit 11, Water (Y5) Unit 23, Investigating coasts (Y5/6) Unit 25, Geography and numbers (Y1–6)	art and design, history, design and technology, music
	5E. Earth, sun, moon (Y5)		art, music, PE, dance
Music	9. Animal Magic (Y3/4) 13. Painting with sound (Y3/4)	Unit 7, Weather around the world (Y3) Unit 18, Connecting Ourselves to the World (Y3–6)	science, history, art, ICT PE, dance
	14. Salt,Pepper, Vinegar, Mustard (Y3/4)	Unit 6, Investigating our local area (Y3)	
Religious Education	3B. How and Why do Hindus celebrate Divali? (Y3/4) 4A. How and Why do Hindus worship at home and in the mandir? (Y3/4)	Unit 6, Investigating our local area (Y3)	history, art and design, design and technology, music, ICT, PE, dance
	4D. What religions are represented in our neighbourhood? (Y3/4)	Unit 10, A village in India (Y4)	
	5A. Why is Muhammad important to Muslims? (Y5/6) 5B. How do Muslims express their beliefs through practices?	Unit 6, Investigating our local area (Y3) Unit 18, Connecting ourselves with the world (Y3–6)	art and design, music
	6B. What is the role of the mosque? 6D. What is the Qur'an and why is it important to Muslims? (Y5/6)	Unit 13, A contrasting UK locality (Y5) Unit 9, Village settlers (Y4)	
	6F. How do people express their faith through the arts? (Y5/6)	Unit 6, Investigating our local area (Y3)	art and design, PE, dance, music
History	6A. Why have people settled in and invaded Britain in the past? A Roman case study or an Anglo-Saxon or Viking case study (Y3/4)		art and design, music, design and technology, science

11. What was it like living in Victorian Britain? Or 12. How did life change in our locality in Victorian times? Or 13. How has life in Britain changed since 1948? (Y5/6) 16. What can we find out about the Indus Valley Civilization? (Y5/6) 18. What was it like to live here in the past? (Y3/4) 19. What were the effects of Tudor explorations? (Y6)	Unit 10, A village in India (Y4) Unit 6, Investigating our local area (Y3) Unit 24, A passport to the world (Y1–6)	art and design, music,
Art and Design 3B. Investigating Pattern (e.g. Indian printed textiles, Islamic tiles, Bengali kanthas work, Scandinavian designs, Asofo work from Ghana) (Y3/4) 3C. Can we change places please? (e.g. maps and plans of different types of location; use of 'found' materials) (Y3/4) 4B. Take a Seat (e.g. examples of chairs from different cultures) (Y3/4) 4C. Journeys (e.g. aerial photographs, ancient and modern maps, weather maps) (Y3/4) 5B. Containers (e.g. vessels and containers of different sorts) (Y5/6) 5C. Talking Textiles (e.g. textiles or photographs of textiles; embroidered shrine cloth from northern India, Chinese ceramics) (Y5/6)	Unit 10, A village in India (Y4) Unit 13, A contrasting locality overseas (Y5) Unit 11, Water (Y5) Unit 6, Investigating our local area (Y3) Unit 7, Weather around the world (Y3) Unit 13, A contrasting UK locality (Y5) Unit 18, Connecting ourselves to the world (Y3/6) Unit 24, A Passport to the world (Y1/6) Unit 13, A contrasting UK locality (Y5)	science science design and technology science, design and technology science design and technology, ICT

Subject	Scheme	Geography scheme links	Possible links to other subjects
	6A. People in Action (e.g. sport dance music from other times, places) (Y5/6) 6C. A sense of place (e.g. photographs from urban and rural landscapes) (Y5/6)		science, religious education, PE, dance, music
Physical Education	2. Outdoor and adventurous activities (e.g. use maps to orientate selves and travel a short route) (Y3/4) 5. Dance activities (Y5) 6. Dance activities (Y6) Dance Activities, link (Y6/7)	Unit 6, Investigating the local area (Y3) Unit 19, How and where do we spend our time? (Y4) Unit 10, A village in India (Y4) Unit 11, Water (Y5) Unit 6, Investigating rivers (Y6) Unit 15, The mountain environment (Y6) Unit 18, Connecting ourselves to the World (Y3/6) Unit 22, A passport to the world (Y1/6)	music PE
Design and Technology	5A. Musical Instruments (e.g. including instruments from other times and cultures) (Y5) 6A. Shelters (e.g. bridges) (Y6)	Unit 10, A village in India (Y4) Unit 19, Connecting ourselves to the world (Y3/6) Unit 24, Passport to the world (Y1/6)	

FIGURE 10.6 Examples of additional links between geography and other QCA schemes of work (excluding English and mathematics which can be developed through any Unit)

well as vocabulary lists for each subject. Learning outcomes for each subject need to be modified and linked to the learning objectives; sometimes these can be combined.

Inversely, co-ordinators for other subjects could take the initiative and consider, from their perspectives, how their subjects can be linked to geography as suggested in Figure 10.6.

Different types of subject links

The values and thinking skills, interpreted in the context of geography at the beginning of this chapter and the links between geography and other subjects can be referenced to the National Curriculum Handbook. English, mathematics and ICT, although taught and planned for discretely, are communication systems which can also be applied and made meaningful in the context of any topic being taught.

Music and art and design are based on a spiralling of skills and processes applied to broad areas of study. In geography and history, however, there is specified content in the statutory curriculum. Some schools therefore, aiming at a more integrated curriculum at Key Stage 2, plan in the long term for specific linked geography and history topics, either combined or sequential. It is possible then, at a medium-term level, either to allow Year group teams or individual teachers to make links between the geography or history topic and music, art and design and technology in flexible and creative ways, allowing children to make their own suggestions.

All the required knowledge, skills and understanding in each subject need to be taken into account, with whole-school monitoring of the breadth of study covered, and modifications where necessary. This provides flexibility and opportunities for teachers and children to experiment, review and develop a holistic curriculum, responding to what the children enjoy.

References

Akester, H., Double, H., Hill, R. and Wright, L. (2005) 'Walkie talkie', *Primary Geographer*, Spring, 26–7.

Baker, K. (ed.) (2000) *The Faber Book of Landscape Poetry*. London: Faber and Faber.

Barnard, N. (2005) 'Good rate of exchange', *Times Educational Supplement, The Teacher*, 6 May, 6–7.

Barnes, J. (2004) 'Geography, creativity and place', in Scoffham, S. (ed.) *Primary Geography Handbook*. Sheffield: Geographical Association.

Binch, N. and Clive, S. (1994) *Close Collaborations: Art in Schools and the Environment*. London: The Arts Council of England.

Bloom, A. (2005) 'Pupils paint the same picture', *Times Educational Supplement*, 15 April, 12.

Boxer, R. and Walker, K. (2005) 'Where I live', *Primary Geographer*, Spring, 28–9.

Callaway, G. and Kear, M. (1999) *Teaching Art and Design in the Primary School*. London: David Fulton Publishers.

Clement, R. and Page, S. (1992a) *Primary Art. Knowledge and Understanding in Art*. Harlow: Oliver & Boyd.

Clement, R. and Page, S. (1992b) *Primary Art. Investigating and Making in Art*. Harlow: Oliver & Boyd.

DES (1989) *National Curriculum: from policy to practice*. London: HMSO.

DES/WO (1990) *Geography for Ages 5 to 16*. London: HMSO.

DfEE (1998) *The National Literacy Strategy*. London: DfEE.

DfEE (1999) *The National Numeracy Strategy*. London: DfEE.

DfEE/QCA (1999) *The National Curriculum: handbook for primary teachers in England*. London: QCA, www.nc.uk.net

DfES (2003) *Excellence and Enjoyment: A Strategy for Primary Schools*. London: DfES, www.standards.dfes.gov.uk

Gardner, H. (1993) (2ⁿᵈ edn) *Frances of Mind: The Theory of Multiple Intelligences*. London: Fontana.

Goleman, D. (1996) *Emotional Intelligence: Why it can matter more than IQ*. London: Bloomsbury.

Halstead, J. M. (1997) 'Educating the human spirit: an appraisal of the spiritual dimension of primary arts education', in *Primary Arts Education: Contemporary Issues* ed. D. Holt. London: Falmer.

Hockney, D. (2004) *Hockney's Pictures*. New York: Bullfinch Press.

Iwaskow, L. (2005) 'Walking the green walk', *Times Educational Supplement*, 21 January, 23.

Jackson, E. (2004) 'Citizenship, PSHE and primary geography', in Scoffham, S. (ed.) *Primary Geography Handbook*. Sheffield: Geographical Association.

Keeping, C. (1989) *Adam and Paradise Island*. Oxford: Oxford University Press.

Lepkowska, D. (2005) 'A leaf out of Africa's book', *Times Educational Supplement*, 8 April, 17.

Mackintosh, M. (2005) 'Talking about "the last wilderness" ', *Primary Geography*, Spring, 32–4.

Meager, N. and Ashfield, J. (1997) *Teaching Art at Key Stage 2*. Wiltshire: National Society for Education in Art.

Monahan, J. (2005) 'Life on the edge', *Times Educational Supplement, The Teacher*, 30, 14 October.

Ord, W. (2005) 'Small thinking must think big', *Times Educational Suplement*, 21 January, 23.

Plowden, B. (1967) *Children and their Primary Schools*. London: HMSO.

QCA (2000) *A Scheme of Work for Key Stages 1 and 2*. London: QCA.

QCA (2005) *Futures: meeting the challenge*. London: QCA, www.qca.org.uk

Richards, G. (2005) 'Access the world', *Times Educational Supplement, The Teacher*, 4 February, 29.

Robertson, M. (2005) Now and Then: The poetry of Martin Robertson, http://rtn.uk/org/now_and_then

Rowley, C. and Lewis, L. (2003) *Thinking on the Edge*. London: Living Earth.

Scoffham, S. (ed.) (2004) *Primary Geography Handbook*. Sheffield: Geographical Association.

Swift, D. and Lambert, D. (2005) 'Swept up together', *Times Educational Supplement, The Teacher*, 4 February, 22.

Thomas, A. (2005) 'A breath of the Continent', *Times Educational Supplement, The Teacher*, 6 May, 22.

Tremlett, G. (2003) 'Summer holiday Shackletons put Antarctica in peril', *Guardian*, 18 June.

Weblinks

www.globalgateway.org

www.britishcouncil.org/globalschools

www.qca.org.uk/geography

www.greenlighttrust.org

www.artpromote.com/ethnic.shtml

www.aklowa.net

http://bbc.co.uk/worldclass/

www.MakeTheLink@tes.co.uk

www.empiremuseum.co.uk

www.nmafasa.si.exhibits/

www.virtualmuseum.ca/Exhibitions/Landscapes/

Global issues and campaigns

Make poverty history www.makepovertyhistory.org/education.html

Send my friend to school www.sendmyfriend.org/

Global Campaign for Education www.campaignforeducation.org/

Development Education Association www.globaldimension.org.uk

International Broadcasting Trust www.ibt.org.uk

The Rough Guide to a Better World www.roughguide-betterworld.com

UN global issues resource www.un.org/Pubs/CyberSchoolBus/

www.commissionforAfrica.org

www.learningafrica.org.uk

www.sendmyfriend.org

Art, music, places and landscapes

www.ambleside.schoolzone.co.uk

www.earth.google.com

www.tate.org.uk

www.tuned-in.org

www.virtualmuseum.ca/Exhibitions/Landscapes/

www.artpromote.com/ethnic.shtml (Ethnic arts from around the world)

www.artpromote.com/african.shtml

www.nmafa.si.edu (Smithsonian National Museum of African Art)

http://www.eartheducation.org/resource.asp?sku=bek Earthkeepers Four Keys for Helping Young People Live in Harmony with the Earth. Matre, S.V. and Johnson, B., Institute of Education.

Reflections on teaching geography

Neil Simco

IN THIS FINAL chapter I intend to identify and consider the major themes that permeate the book. I regard this as an important task, as together these themes will add up to a set of values or beliefs which define the collective thinking within the book.

Essentially then, this chapter is about clarification, summary and conclusion. However there is more than this. Fundamentally it is concerned with the potential of geography in primary education to transform individuals, communities and society. It argues that geographical education has the potential to reach into rich educative processes which facilitate deep learning in both the cognitive and affective domains.

I shall attempt to develop a number of distinctive phases. Firstly I shall consider the concept of reflection as I wish to suggest that the notion of reflection underpins this book. Here I plan, briefly, to describe some key elements of reflection in education and outline how they relate to the book and to the concepts involved in teaching primary geography. Then I want to consider how a generic consideration of reflection relates to the three key themes running through this text. Next I wish to move into the main part of the chapter, which will use exemplars from the book to consider the permitting circumstances for reflection within geographical learning in primary education. The reason why I have chosen to give a relatively high profile to this is because it must not be assumed that reflective learning within primary geographical education is unproblematic or automatic. Reflective learning has to involve a complex set of classroom processes, the realisation of which demands considerable professional skill on the part of the teacher and considerable intellectual and emotional engagement on the part of the learner. I will conclude by considering why these circumstances are significant and important for children's learning.

Three key themes

In preparation for writing this chapter I met with a number of authors of other chapters and through a seminar we identified three major cross-cutting themes in the text.

- Helping children to make sense of the world around them through geographical enquiry

By this I mean a process where children understand more of local and global contexts, both in intellectual and affective ways. This links powerful concepts such as interdependence and environmental sustainability. It also relates to a concept where learners recognise the juxtaposition between themselves and the world.

- Identifying a broad spectrum of enquiry

This involves a recognition that geographical enquiry is multifaceted. There is a clear spectrum from formal scientific enquiry to rich open questioning, from a quantitative to a qualitative approach, from deductive to inductive. This notion is well established but the book, in general, upholds the place of non-scientific enquiry. It suggests that enquiry related to emotional and spiritual connectedness to place can lead the learner to glean transformative understandings. The book argues for an inclusive approach to stimulating curiosity.

- Cross-curricular nature of geography

In many ways this is a book about children's learning, not about a curriculum subject. It argues that geographical learning is, at its core, about children's learning. It is about how children develop intellectually, socially, emotionally and spiritually. The richness of a broadly-based approach to geographical enquiry is related to the richness of a 'whole person' approach to children's learning.

I will return to these themes in more detail later, but in essence, they put geographical learning at the heart of children's learning, and this sits uneasily with the relative demise of geography as a subject area within primary education. Nonetheless, as Simon Asquith points out in Chapter 1, the subject is benefiting from discussion at national level in regard to the place of geography within the Foundation Stage, and Key Stages 1 and 2. For the authors of this book the 'bottom line' is that geographical education and generic child development go hand in hand. It argues for the widespread acceptance of the transformative potential of geography within primary education.

Reflective teaching and learning

I now want to consider how the book relates to the broad themes of reflective teaching. Here the basic tenet is that reflective teaching is, effectively, a necessary but not sufficient condition for reflective learning. If teaching is not reflective and iterative, then it is likely that ensuing learning will be bland, limited and dull. But reflective teaching involves complex processes. There are a number of circumstances which make reflective teaching and learning possible. In order to identify these, a number of factors can be considered.

Diverse knowledge bases

There needs to be an understanding of the diverse range of knowledge that a teacher requires and how this relates to the creation of a reflective classroom. Being an expert teacher – an expert facilitator of learning – requires different kinds of knowledge, ranging from knowledge of the subject area to pedagogical knowledge, knowledge of how to teach this effectively.

There also needs to be consideration of the fine-grain interaction in the classroom, because it is at the level of individual learning exchanges between teachers and pupils, and between pupils, that the reflective classroom is defined. The classroom is a naturalistic environment made up of hundreds of individual learning interactions every day. Just as the knowledge base of the teacher is important for classroom interaction, so too is the ecology of the classroom, a social and psychological dynamic between teachers and pupils (Doyle 1977). Together with the knowledge bases of teachers, classroom ecology provides a context for reflective teaching and learning.

Reflection on teaching

Turner-Bisset (2001) draws together relevant literature on diverse knowledge bases for effective teaching: subject knowledge, curriculum knowledge, general pedagogical knowledge, knowledge about models of teaching, knowledge of learners, knowledge of self, of educational contexts and of educational ends, purposes and values. Drawing on Shulman (1986), Turner-Bisset argues that taken together all these knowledge bases lead to a complex amalgam called pedagogical content knowledge: 'the pedagogical content knowledge of the expert teacher is the set that comprises all of the other sets of knowledge bases' (Turner-Bisset 2001: 17). Of the knowledge sets identified by Turner-Bisset, two seem particularly interesting for the purposes of this chapter, although it is important to note that reflective processes can also be apparent within all of the knowledge bases identified.

Knowledge of educational ends, purposes and values is seen by Turner-Bisset as involving teaching which goes beyond 'purely utilitarian endeavour' (2001: 17) to teaching that has an eye to the long-term consequence for learning of that teaching. Pollard (2002) identifies this as one of the key attributes of reflective teaching. It may be, for example, that as a teacher you have a view that a long-term purpose of education is to facilitate environmental sustainability or a deep engagement for learners with the physical environment around them.

Reflection on learning

A second kind of knowledge base that appears to be fertile ground for reflective practice is concerned with knowledge of learners. In Turner-Bisset's analysis, knowledge of learners consists both of the knowledge of individual learners within the classroom context and of general learning theory about how learners develop and flourish. In order to facilitate reflective learning, it is important to understand how children learn, cognitively, socially and intellectually. This theme is taken further below where there is exploration of the reflective classroom and the juxtaposition between reflective teaching and reflective learning.

If the knowledge base of the teacher is a prerequisite for the creation of a reflective classroom, then so too is the term identified above called 'classroom ecology'. This relates to the social definition of the classroom environment. It relates to a process whereby classroom activity can be defined and described. One way of conceptualising this is through activity analysis (Simco 1995). Here a classroom can be described as open or closed, with open characteristics being seen as related to ownership of time, space, resources and curriculum, for example. The more the pupils are considered to have ownership of the classroom ecology, the more open the classroom environment becomes.

Further, it is possible to define the classroom ecology as being clear or vague, clarity relating, for example, to the extent to which the teacher's instructions are structured and 'pacey'. This definition of classroom ecology leads to classrooms being defined in one of four ways, open-clear, open-closed, closed-clear and closed-vague. Open-clear classrooms are ones where the pupils have some say over the definition of task, the allocation of resources and time and where the teacher manages this in such a way that there is clarity, structure and pace. Closed-clear classrooms are ones where these characteristics of clarity structure and pace remain, but the ownership of the classroom ecology is very much with the teacher. Open-vague classrooms have characteristics of pupils 'owning' the learning agenda, but in a context where there is a lack of structure within the learning. Closed-vague classrooms are ones where not only does the teacher own the learning agenda but this is implemented in such a way that there is a distinct lack of structure and pace.

It is clear that some types of classroom ecology are more facilitative of reflection than others. Closed-vague classrooms have characteristics of a learning context that does not engage children's learning and, even worse, lacks direction for the implementation of the curriculum. On the other hand, open-clear classrooms are ones where not only do children have ownership of their learning, but the teacher manages this learning so that there is a clear structure, direction and pace. It is arguably in these classrooms that there is most likelihood of both reflective teaching and reflective learning. If children have ownership of their learning, then they are most likely to be successful within geographical enquiry as long as the teacher has the ability to manage this learning carefully and skilfully.

Drawing together these concepts of classroom ecology and professional knowledge bases, the importance of these to the notion of the reflective classroom can be identified. Put simply, a classroom characterised by openness and clarity is more likely to be a reflective classroom than one characterised by closedness and vagueness. Pupils need to be free to engage with learning, to author their own geographical enquiry, but to do so within an environment that is both supportive and challenging. In order to manage learning within a classroom environment that has these characteristics, the teacher has to have a professional knowledge base that recognises the skill of managing learning rather than providing direct input, and the skill of doing this in such a way that provides structure to learning, without 'taking over' that learning.

The analysis above establishes, then, that the characteristics of the classroom ecology and the professional knowledge bases of teachers are necessary but not sufficient conditions for reflective teaching. Moreover, if one assumes that reflective teaching is a necessary but not sufficient condition for reflective learning, then it is worthwhile to identify the key characteristics of reflective teaching.

Links between reflective teaching and reflective learning

Pollard (2002) draws on the very extensive literature on reflective teaching to identify seven key characteristics of reflective teaching. I now move on to present and comment on these and create links between the notion of reflective teaching and reflective learning. This point is important because it suggests that there is an inevitable link between reflective teaching and reflective learning. Both notions play off each other and are essentially interdependent. If teachers are reflective in their practice, it is highly likely that pupils will be reflective in their own learning.

This link between reflective teaching and reflective learning is related to the idea behind this book; the subject of geography is very closely related to generic child development.

Geographical enquiry involves processes which are central to cognitive and affective development. It involves learning processes which require framing questions, developing these through interaction with others, gathering evidence and then using this to develop 'new' understanding and learning. It involves a developing sense of place and the idea that place is central to human existence. This clearly relates to learning theory, and in particular Vygotskian models, but for the purposes of this chapter I wish to focus on the precise link between reflective teaching and reflective learning. This can be explored through the creation of a framework that links reflective teaching and reflective learning based on the seven Pollard maxims. Often this link will be implicit rather than explicit and the learning maxims will be expressed through the perspective of children at various stages of their development as people.

Characteristics of reflective teaching

Concern with aims and consequences

'Reflective teaching implies an active concern with aims and consequences' (Pollard 2002: 14). This involves the teacher going beyond the immediate expedient to consider the long-term purposes of education and pupil learning. It involves engagement with issues such as the identification of the underpinning beliefs and values that a teacher has about their teaching and the purposes of education. Likewise a concept of reflective learning can be developed whereby pupils have an explicit awareness of the longer-term learning gains from their work. Within the context of geographical enquiry it is possible for children to understand the relationship between their enquiry and the realisation of a sustainable local ecology for example.

Cyclical review

'Reflective teaching is applied in a cyclical or spiralling process, in which teachers monitor, evaluate and revise their own practice continuously' (Pollard 2002: 14). Here there is a notion of action research and constant evaluation. It is concerned with a continuous process of reflection-on-action (Schon 1983), where continuous improvement is sought through ongoing reflection. It relates to the notion of an active concern with aims and consequences as it is the way in which beliefs and values held about education are actually translated into practice. In terms of reflective learning, this relates to children being involved in critiquing their own work so as to ensure that, through self-awareness of their own learning, they take some responsibility for enhancing their own practice.

Evidence-based classroom enquiry

'Reflective teaching requires competence in methods of evidence-based classroom enquiry, to support the progressive development of higher standards of teaching' (Schon 1983: 14). This is particularly interesting within the context of this book. Several authors of chapters consider the notion of geographical enquiry as the essence of geographical learning for young children. To approach teaching in a way that has enquiry at its centre seems important if there is to be a strong sense of reflective learning within the classroom. Reflective teaching is not only about formal classroom enquiry, but is also about a concept of enquiry underpinning all teaching activity. In some respects, then, this maxim relates most closely to the notion of reflective learning. It demands that pupils have a range of approaches to geographical enquiry that are developed over time.

Open-minded, wholehearted, responsible

This is, for me, the most significant aspect of reflective teaching. Pollard (2002: 14) takes these three words from Dewey's (1933) definitions and considers that alongside the need for skill in reflection and an approach to teaching which takes the long-term view, it is also important to have an approach which enables the permitting circumstances for reflection. Open-mindedness, then, is concerned with openness to educational alternatives while wholeheartedness marks a clear and positive commitment to the educational function. Responsibility involves an acknowledgement of the nature of education as being important for the formation of individuals, for communities and society. In relation to learning, it suggests that it is more likely that learners will be reflective if they too have attitudes to learning characterised by open-mindedness, wholeheartedness and responsibility, namely an openness to alternative in the enquiry process, a wholehearted commitment to that process and a recognition that the outcomes of enquiry may make a positive contribution to the development of the local community for example.

Informed teacher judgement

'Reflective teaching is based on teacher judgement, informed by evidence-based enquiry and insights from other research' (Pollard 2002: 14). This is the first of two maxims that suggest that reflection should not be a lone activity! It involves inter-action with evidence from research. Sometimes this is hard to achieve in the cut and thrust of classroom life, and government policy mandates. Nonetheless it does demand a responsiveness to educational research of various kinds. It is also challenging to educational researchers who do not always communicate their work in a way that is accessible to busy practitioners. For pupils, this maxim is concerned with the extent to which their learning relates to the learning of others. In pursing a geographical enquiry through the citation of a number of questions, to what extent is that enquiry related to the findings of others both within and beyond the specific learning environment under question?

Collaboration with colleagues

'Reflective teaching, professional learning and personal fulfilment are enhanced through collaboration and dialogue with colleagues' (Pollard 2002: 14). This is the second of two maxims that relate to reflective teaching occurring in an interactive context. Just as geographical enquiry is enhanced through young children engaging in various forms of dialogue and interaction, so it is with reflective teaching. The essence of the reflective process is two or more colleagues talking with each other in a way that facilitates the realisation of fresh insights into classroom processes and excellence in learning. Therefore interaction is essential in learning whether through formal structured discussion or through, say, informal interaction in the field. It celebrates the principle that reflective learning is a dynamic process rooted in moment by moment interaction between learners.

Developing given frameworks

'Reflective teaching enables teachers to creatively mediate externally developed frameworks for teaching and learning' (Pollard 2002: 15). This final construct is concerned with a recognition that teachers can respond to external initiatives in a way that modifies them to apply to the particular circumstances of individual classrooms. This has become particularly important in recent years. Since New Labour came to power in 1997, there has been a proliferation of initiatives (particular the literacy and numeracy strategies) which created a sense among some that teacher professionalism had been compromised in the face of an imposed mandate. Pollard's suggestion is that reflective teaching is a way that teachers can be creative in relating these initiatives to their own contexts, beliefs and values.

Reflection within geographical learning

I have considered the generic characteristics of the reflective classroom and have identified some generic circumstances which make it possible to put these into practice. Building on this, I now wish to consider reflection within geographical learning which arise from various chapters in the book. In doing this I aim to make some key links between the Pollard (2002) characteristics of reflective practice and the central themes that run through the book.

Personal geographies

The Catling (2003) notion of children's personal geographies is picked up by a number of authors, particularly Simon Asquith and Chris Rowley and interestingly relates to the open-closed dimension of the classroom ecology discussed above, because personal geographies are by definition concerned with children owning their own senses of place. Geographies are related to the sense of place that children bring into their geographical learning. They are about pupils' understanding of the characteristics of place, particularly local place. Moreover, Asquith argues that these personal geographies can often be the creative spark for learning. He contrasts this with an approach to learning whereby the ownership of this rests with the teacher who may fail to really understand the intricacies of children's personal geographies and the complex and detailed sense of place, particularly local place, that all children will have.

The reflective classroom has to be one where children's personal geographies are acknowledged within geographical enquiry because this is about openness in learning. Enquiry that arises out of, or is someway related to children's sense of place, is likely to have strong elements of reflection because it is a context that is deeply meaningful to children. In essence, the reflective classroom is about the children's agenda and within geography the essence of the children's agenda has to be their personal geographies.

A diverse and inclusive approach to geographical enquiry

Geographical enquiry is at the centre of the teaching and learning of the subject in primary schools. It is concerned with what questions pupils ask, how these questions are stimulated and subsequently how they are carried through. Given the importance of enquiry, it is inevitable that this notion must be considered in any analysis of the reflective classroom.

Chris Rowley challenges us to think in terms of a diversity of enquiry. He suggests that variants of deductive scientific enquiry are prevalent in primary education and, while appropriate, these approaches are not sufficient. Particularly important is the acknowledgement that should be given to creative enquiry that derives from children's own curiosity. This relates to the generic theme of the reflective classroom being an open classroom where there is recognition of the educational validity of a range of approaches. This is also important in the sense of an acknowledgement of approaches to differentiation and personalised learning and this is an agenda that is picked up by Justine Slaymaker who considers an approach to geography that includes all children, particularly those with special educational needs. Children's personal geographies can be brought out through a broad approach to enquiry that strengthens the extent to which the classroom is both open and responsive. Rowley also encourages us to consider geographical enquiry as both aesthetic and ethical and these two aspects are picked up by Kevin Hamel and Katharine Langley-Hamel as they consider these elements in their study of teaching distant place through story and music. Sophie Mackay, Gina Mullarkey and Vimala John also consider the global dimension from the perspective of development education.

In this way the reflective classroom is enhanced and deepened because as part of their geographical learning pupils have the opportunity to deal with geographical questions in a diverse way.

Bridging the gap between knowing and enquiry and being able to use enquiry effectively within geographical teaching

Teaching geographical enquiry well is both challenging and important. Referring back to the Pollard maxims, it involves, on the part of both the teacher and the learner, a constant process of evaluation and review, a cyclical process of reflection and continuous improvement. This book asserts that not only is geographical enquiry central to geographical education, but that geographical enquiry is a broadly-based concept ranging from scientific approaches to approaches which respond to children's curiosity about place. To be able to teach in such a way that embraces this diversity is demanding indeed.

A number of contributors to this book identify the limitations of more traditional quasi-scientific or rational approaches to enquiry. Rowley, for example, cites the Storm (1989) questions and how these have been misinterpreted by some, with implications that enquiry becomes descriptive and closed as opposed to reflective and open. John Goodwin identifies the limitations of QCA schemes of work and reminds us of the need for an approach to geographical teaching that is innovative and creative, rather than mechanistic and dull. To learn to teach enquiry effectively demands a rich professional knowledge base, that joins knowledge about learners and learning to knowledge about pedagogical approaches centred on openness and responsiveness to children's curiosity.

An emotionally intelligent approach to geographical enquiry

This concept of emotional as opposed to rational engagement with place is developed in various places through the book, most notably in Chris Buxton's chapter. His words sum up the criticality of emotional engagement with place.

> 'Children need the opportunity to really connect to and love a place . . . That bond with a deep and natural part of our being can provide the motivation to want to act to care for the local place and the wider world beyond (deep emotional literacy), as well as to develop the understanding of how it works and our role in it (deep ecological 'literacy'). Without emotional affection for our own place, why should we be interested in caring for anyone else's place?'

Part of Buxton's thinking relates to the critical importance of local fieldwork and the desirability of immersing self in place. This in turn links to the Pollard reflective maxims around open-mindedness, wholeheartedness and responsibility and provides an indication as to how emotional literacy links with reflective practice. In particular, wholeheartedness intrinsically has an emotional dimension as it implies a strong engagement with reflective learning. Dewey (1933: 30) suggests that 'A genuine enthusiasm is an attitude that operates as an intellectual force. When a person is absorbed, the subject carries him on.' To immerse self in place as part of geographical enquiry is both a reflective activity and a wholehearted one.

Hilary Cooper is also concerned with this area of the reflective classroom in her consideration of how young children develop a spiritual sense of place through engagement with geographical enquiry. Children know and understand that some places are special to them and that these places will have a deep and profound connection to their inner-selves and a sense, perhaps of awe and wonder. Taken together, emotional and spiritual intelligence are fertile ground to explore the geographically reflective classroom.

An integrated approach to the curriculum and a holistic approach to child development

One of the Pollard maxims is concerned with an active concern with aims and consequences, as well as means and technical efficiency. If aims and consequences are at least as significant as means, then it is also true that the boundaries of the curriculum are perhaps less important than a holistic approach to children's learning, which has aims and consequences very much at the centre. Education is, first and foremost, about the education of the person, rather than the celebration of the subject. Ultimately then, to be reflective requires an approach that crosses boundaries of specific subjects.

Geographical learning is perhaps uniquely placed to be integrated with other subjects for the benefit of a holistic approach to pupils' learning and a number of authors provide detail and exemplars of this. Nigel Toye and Denise Evans' chapter is focused on the role of drama. They suggest an approach that starts from the children and asks the crucially important questions about how we engage with them. They identify the importance of experiential learning and use drama to enable children to connect to a distant place. They suggest that the use of pictures to facilitate children's engagement with a distant place is necessarily limited. This can, of course, be linked with the Pollard notion of the importance of interaction in a reflective classroom.

Building on Jan Ashbridge's integrated approach to geography at the Foundation Stage, Kevin Hamel and Katharine Langley-Hamel illustrate the contribution of geography to the whole Key Stage 1 curriculum. This is explored in particular through an approach that identifies the place of narrative and the sounds of places through narrative. The chapter is illustrated by rich data drawn from a comparative study of children from Manchester and from Cumbria. The chapter has synergy with Nigel Toye and Denise Evans' work as it again affirms a focus on the child rather than the subject: indeed the actual title of the chapter is the contribution geography makes to a 'coherent and meaningful' Key Stage 1 curriculum, coherent and meaningful in the sense that there is a clear and defined focus on children's learning as a holistic concept. Hilary Cooper takes this a step further by providing material at Key Stage 2 which illustrates the key connections between geography and a wide range of subjects within the National Curriculum.

The main thing that links all of these permitting circumstances is an aspiration for a reflective classroom, developed, in particular, through geographical education. This is important because geography as a subject area is in a powerful place, perhaps the most powerful place to transform individuals, communities and society. Geography is about facilitating children's understanding of place. It is also about developing children's understanding of their affective and cognitive engagement with place. It is about ensuring that children care about place, local and global and it is concerned about how places change and what impact human activity has on place.

Ultimately, geography is about education for sustainability, the sustainability of the environment and the sustainability of communities and individuals within our world.

It follows that a reflective classroom provides an environment where geographical enquiry can flourish. Yet a reflective classroom cannot be taken for granted. It demands a classroom ecology characterised by openness and clarity, where pupils have ownership of their own learning and where curiosity is nurtured, encouraged and celebrated. It also demands an approach to teaching characterised by attitudes of open-mindedness, wholeheartedness and responsibility, by a striving for continuous improvement based on evaluation, reflection and action research and by constant interaction between professionals and with pupils. To achieve all of this is indeed demanding for teachers. Not only do they have to have an understanding of the nature of the subject and its contribution to the curriculum, but they need to have a professional knowledge base which can be deployed, moment by moment, in the complexity of the classroom ecology, in order to realise a diverse approach to geographical enquiry. Put simply, this book is about a passion for geography, a greater passion for education and an even greater passion for the transformative role of learning.

References

Catling, S. (2003) 'Curriculum contested: Primary geography and social justice', *Geography*, **88** (3), 164–210.

Dewey, J. (1933) *How We Think: A Restatement of the Relation of Reflective Thinking to the Educative Process*. Chicago: Henry Regnery.

Doyle, W. (1977) 'Learning the classroom environment: an ecological analysis', *Journal of Teacher Education*, **XXV111** (6), 51–4.

Pollard, A. (2002) *Reflective Teaching*, 2nd edn. London: Continuum.

Schon, D. (1983) *The Reflective Practitioner: How Professionals think in Action*. London: Temple Smith.

Shulman, L. S. (1986) 'Those who understand: knowledge growth in teaching', *Educational Researcher*, **15** (2), 4–14.

Simco, N. (1995), 'Using activity analysis to investigate primary classroom environments', *British Education Research Journal*, 21(1): 49-60.

Storm, M. (1989) 'The five basic questions for primary geography', *Primary Geographer*, **2**, 4–5.

Turner-Bisset, R. (2001) *Expert Teaching: Knowledge and Pedagogy to Lead the Profession*. London: David Fulton Publishers.

Index